W9-BFC-973

THE SPIRIT LED WOMAN

Compiled by J. W. Martin

CREATION HOUSE

THE SPIRITLED WOMAN
Published by Creation House
Strang Communications Company
600 Rinehart Road
Lake Mary, Florida 32746
www.creationhouse.com
www.charismalife.com

Unless otherwise noted, all Scripture quotations are from the King James Version of the Bible.

Scripture quotations marked AMP are from the Amplified Bible. Old Testament copyright © 1965, 1987 by the Zondervan Corporation. The Amplified New Testament copyright © 1954, 1958, 1987 by the Lockman Foundation. Used by permission.

Scripture quotations marked TLB are from The Living Bible. Copyright © 1971. Used by permission of Tyndale House Publishers, Inc., Wheaton, IL 60189. All rights reserved.

Scripture quotations marked NKJV are from the New King James Version of the Bible. Copyright © 1979, 1980, 1982 by Thomas Nelson, Inc., publishers. Used by permission.

Interior design by Lillian L. McAnally

ISBN: 0-88419-660-7

This book was formerly published as *The Spirit-Filled Woman,* copyright © 1997 by Creation House, ISBN 0-88419-483-3.

Printed in the United States of America

Dedicated . . .

To the women who have gone before—
Pioneers.
Trail-blazers.
Victorious women.
Virtuous women of prayer and fasting.
Godly women whose tears of intercession watered the way
    for those of us who are Spirit-led women today.

Contents

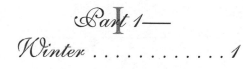

Part 1—
Winter *1*

Part 2—
Spring *81*

Part 3—
Summer *160*

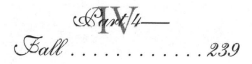

Part 4—
Fall *239*

Introduction

I have always been a person who enjoyed being by herself. My first response when I feel pressed by the overwhelming responsibilities I face almost daily is to get alone. That is the way I regenerate.

In reality, though, I'm never alone during my times of regrouping. I generally spend them praying and communing with the Lord, or reading—and then I am in the company of the great heroes of the faith who have gone before me and blazed a path for me to follow.

I especially enjoy reading books by or about Spirit-led women. Their lives inspire me, and the timeless wisdom they express gives me insight for my own spiritual journey. Women such as Phoebe Palmer, Maria Woodworth-Etter, and Carrie Judd Montgomery set a powerful example for me of what God can do through one person who is totally committed to Him. In times when it was, if not unheard of, at least very unpopular, to be a woman preacher, these women stepped out in faith to lay hold of the call of God and allow the Holy Spirit to touch the world through them. What they did required not only unwavering faith but also tremendous commitment and a determination to please God in spite of the opinions of others.

I believe we can all draw from the experiences and teachings of these godly women. Because God is the same yesterday, today, and forever, the truths they learned on their Christian walks are as applicable in our day as they were in theirs. And the words the Holy Spirit spoke through them are words He has been speaking to God's people since the foundation of the world. These words are therefore not anachronisms, as some may think, but prophetic messages that can enlighten the hearts and minds of Spirit-led women today as surely as they did the hearts and minds of women in previous ages.

The Bible tells us that "every scribe which is instructed unto the kingdom of heaven is like unto a man that is an householder, which bringeth forth out of his treasure things new and old" (Matt. 13:52). I am very grateful for the ministry of modern-day women preachers who have impacted my life at a deep level and who are available to touch other women around the world in a personal way. Many of them speak at our *Charisma* Women's Conferences and write for *SpiritLed Woman* magazine. They are "new treasure" we would not want to be without.

But there is great value in learning from women of the past—drawing from the "old treasure" that is in the storehouse. As we see the incredible ways in which God used these women and read their responses to His action in their lives, we are encouraged to believe that He can and will use us for great things, also. We are emboldened to reach out to embrace the call He has on our lives and begin to cooperate with Him in fulfilling it. We are inspired to become women of destiny who know we were created for kingdom purposes and who are determined to carry out those purposes.

I pray that the old treasure represented on these pages will inspire you to lay hold of your destiny and allow God to do mighty works through you. May you see Him more clearly as you reflect on the devotions each day throughout the year.

—*Joy F. Strang*
Publisher, SpiritLed Woman *magazine*

Seasons in a Spirit-Led Woman's Life

There are many seasons in the life of every Spirit-led woman. Unlikely as it may seem, the cycle of spiritual seasons does not begin with spring. No, winter is where it actually begins, when the Word of God is first sown in the heart. The spiritual walk begins at spiritual ground zero without any fruit to show for all the initial months of effort. That's when faith is the candle that takes you through the cold, gray days.

Just when the Spirit-led woman feels that she has adjusted to winter and trusing God regardless of whether or not there is fruit to show for it, a bud begins to appear, and then a few blades. Spring has begun to produce a simple crop of fruit from the prayers and the faithful lifestyle that was cloaked in winter's cover.

And when spring has had its cycle, summer presents a bumper crop of results from the seeds of the secret times when all the Spirit-led woman could do was pray and walk and go by faith and trust.

Finally, fall comes—the time to harvest and enjoy a lifetime of bounty from the endless supply of the storehouse of God!

As you read through this devotional each day, devote every day and every season to God. Your faithful obedience will produce a lifetime of blessing and a legacy of godliness—just as it did for those faithful women who went before you.

Part 1—
Winter

To everything there is a season,
A time for every purpose under heaven . . .

—*Ecclesiastes 3:1–2*, NKJV

Week 1—Day 1

Shut to the Door

READ 2 KINGS 4:4, 21; MATTHEW 6:6

Wouldst thou thy Lord in blessing meet—
Wouldst find new strength and uplift sweet?
And tarry at His nail-pierced feet
'Til glory falls thy soul to greet?
Enter thy secret-place, and more—
Shut to the door, shut to the door.

Not in the crowd doth God reveal
The hidden union thou wouldst feel;
No hand of man can ever seal
Thy life with holy impress real,
Enter thy secret-place, and more—
Shut to the door, shut to the door.

Why shut the door? To leave behind
The workings of thy natural mind—
Discouragement, self-pity blind—
God's light with those thou canst not find.
Enter thy secret place, and more—
Shut to the door, shut to the door.

—*Alice Reynolds Flowers*
January 1935

Yes, Lord, help me enter into that secret place of Your Presence—and once I'm there, help me to shut the door. In Jesus' name. Amen.

Golden Grain.

Day 2
Let There Be No Waverings

READ ROMANS 1:16–21

Many indulge in waverings to such a degree that you seldom know where to find them. One day, you may find them in a high state of emotion, professing faith in Christ as their full Savior, and on another, wavering and dispirited. It is because their faith depends on the state of their emotions rather than on the faithfulness of God.

Let there be no waverings. Such a profession dishonors God, and it is only by the self-induced consequences of such a course that those who do thus are driven about, and tossed as a wave of the sea, and do not receive any thing from the hand of the Lord. Remember Romans 1:17: "The just shall live by faith!"

—*Phoebe Palmer*
1855

Lord, anchor my soul in the bedrock of faith so there will be no waverings within me. Teach me, Lord, that it is faith in Christ and not emotions that will produce results. Amen.

Incidental Illustrations of the Economy of Salvation, Its Doctrines and Duties (Boston, MA: S. Chism Franklin Printing House, 1833).

Day 3

A Point Beyond Wavering

READ MARK 16:16

There is a point beyond wavering, and it is that moment when you know that God *cannot* be unfaithful. It is only for you to know that you comply with the condition upon which He promises this blessing of salvation from all sin to know that He, at that moment, fulfills the promise to you. So long as you are empowered by the Holy Spirit to offer yourself a living sacrifice to God through Christ, so long you may know that the offering is holy and acceptable. God has said so, and to doubt it is a sin. It is doubting God, and "He that believeth not maketh God a liar." (See 1 John 5:10.) Awful alternative!

Are you now beyond the point of wavering?

—*Phoebe Palmer*
1855

Lord, help me to reach that point beyond wavering—when I know deep within that You cannot be unfaithful. Teach me to walk by faith . . . and not by my emotions! Amen.

Incidental Illustrations of the Economy of Salvation, Its Doctrines and Duties (Boston, MA: S. Chism Franklin Printing House, 1833).

Day 4

More Precious Than Gold

READ 2 CORINTHIANS 4:17; 1 PETER 1:7

How can trials produce any good thing in us? How can they work together for our good, which is God's promise to us? To the eye of reason, this is indeed difficult to fathom; but through eyes of faith we see enemies scattered, their force broken as their missiles fall harmless at the feet of the faithful servant of God.

The test of faith is more precious than gold. How instructive and inspiring are the words, "That the trial of your faith, being much more precious than of gold that perisheth, though it be tried with fire, might be found unto praise and honor and glory at the appearing of Jesus Christ" 1 Pet. 1:7). You see, Jesus gathers every missile the enemy has aimed at us, and it is He who changes things. Look! Every missile meant for your destruction has been gathered by the Lord and turned to gold—pure gold!

—*Phoebe Palmer*
1855

> *Lord, this is a hard thing for me to ask, but help me to understand the mystery of the test of faith so that when the trials come I can trust You to fight the battle for me. Amen.*

Incidental Illustrations of the Economy of Salvation, Its Doctrines and Duties (Boston, MA: S. Chism Franklin Printing House, 1833).

Day 5
A Higher Form of Love

Read Deuteronomy 7:8

Why do you love God? Because He has given you gifts, prospered you, healed you, and poured His blessings upon you? To many people, religion is the coin that purchases the benefits of God.

Yet, isn't there a higher form of love?

We don't love our children because of their abilities. We love them for themselves. It's the same with our husbands, our fathers, and our mothers; we are grateful for what they have done for us. But we love them for who they are.

When we begin to see who God is and appreciate His person, don't we begin to love Him for Himself also? God wants just one thing from us—that we will learn to love Him for who He is. We must simply love Him because of who He is and because He first loved us—not for what He can provide for us.

—*Roxanne Brandt*
1973

Lord, thank You for Your many blessings—but teach me to love You for who You are, not what You can do for me. Amen.

Ministering to the Lord, (Springdale, PA: Whitaker House, 1973).

Weekend

Believe God for Anything

READ ROMANS 4:18–21

Abraham came to the place where he could believe God for anything. He believed that everything God promised, He was able to perform. Faith considers absolutely nothing but the promise of God. Not circumstances. Not appearances. Not the natural realm. Just God's promises.

Have you given up expecting great things from God, and settled down into an ordinary Christian life, putting off to another age things that God will do right here and now as soon as conditions are met? What are the conditions? Only believe. Believe God for anything. O dear disappointed one, God is wooing you into such a place of close fellowship with Him, to a place of such assurance that you will be able to say to Him: "I know You hear me always! I can believe You for anything!"

—*Margaret N. Gordon*
1917

Lord, thank You that You hear me always. Bring me to the place where I can believe You for anything! Amen.

"Purity in Prayer Life," *The Weekly Evangel.*

Week 2—Day 1

Behold, the Man!

READ JOHN 19:5

Jesus promised in His Word that if He be lifted up, He will draw all men unto Himself. See John 12:32.) With that verse burning in my heart, I cried out to the Lord to help me sink out of sight and lift Him up. Behold, the Man!

Behold, the Man—the only One who can save from sin. Stop beholding your business . . . pleasure . . . neighbors . . . earthly cares and duties. Whatever may be absorbing your attention, stop beholding that thing, and instead, behold, the Man!

Just one glimpse of that glorious face—the fairest among ten thousand—will fill you with gratitude for His supreme sacrifice. Those tender eyes, so filled with understanding, sympathy, and love, will bring tears to your eyes too as you behold Jesus. As the shades of darkness and unbelief are driven back by the light of the sun of righteousness, behold, the Man—until your heart bursts forth with singing.

—*Aimee Semple McPherson*
1923

> *Lord, help me to behold You—and as I do, to appreciate all that You have done for me. I praise You for Your sacrifice of love. Amen.*

"Behold the Man!," *This Is That.* Used by permission of the Heritage Department of the Foursquare Gospel.

Day 2
Dig Deep to Build Higher

READ 1 CORINTHIANS 3:9–17; JAMES 4:6–10

While in New York City, I was much impressed with the world-famous skyscrapers. I watched with fascination as a new skyscraper went up. As I considered the work, the Holy Spirit quickened to me that building one's spiritual life is much the same as building a skyscraper strong enough to withstand the altitude and winds and turbulent weather. The higher the building was destined to one day soar, the deeper the foundation.

So it is with us: We must dig a deep foundation. Then we add humility. Then the blood is applied as we fall prostrate at the feet of Jesus, overcome with the revelation that *the way up* is indeed *the way down*.

Neighbors may laugh and friends may never understand, but keep right on digging deep, watering the foundations with weeping. The greatest builders remove every hindrance to stability by blasting away all the debris. Now, as holiness is formed, you are ready to build higher— and finally, the results of that secret work may be outwardly visible. See? He has exalted you!

—*Aimee Semple McPherson*
1923

Lord, I humble myself before You and ask You to build a deep foundation on the solid Rock of Christ. I praise You that as I humble myself, You will exalt me in due season. Amen.

"Behold the Man!," *This Is That.* Used by permission of the Heritage Department of the Foursquare Gospel.

Day 3

Women of the Gospel

READ ACTS 18:2–18, 26; ROMANS 16

Paul worked with the women of the gospel more than any of the other apostles. Priscilla and Phoebe traveled with him, preaching and building up the churches. Paul and Phoebe had been holding revivals together; now she was called to the city of Rome. Paul could not accompany her, but he was very mindful of her reputation and so wrote a letter of recommendation:

"I commend unto you Phoebe, our sister, which is a servant of the church [which signifies a minister of the church] at Cenchrea: that ye receive her in the Lord, as becometh saints, and that ye assist her in whatsoever business she hath need of you: for she has been a succourer of many, and of myself also" (Rom. 16:1).

This shows she had authority to do business in the churches, and that she had been successful in winning souls to Christ. Paul is not ashamed to say she had encouraged him; he speaks of her in the highest praise.

So let it be said of us.

—Maria Woodworth-Etter
1916

Father, I praise You for the women of the gospel and for Paul the Apostle. I thank You for those who have gone before to blaze the trail so that I can now minister Your Word. Amen.

"Women's Right in the Gospel," *Signs and Wonders.*

Day 4
Shining Lights for Christ

READ MATTHEW 5:14–16

Sisters in Christ, it is high time for women to let their lights shine; to bring out their talents that have been hidden away rusting and use them for the glory of God; and do with their might what their hands find to do, trusting God for strength, who has said, "I will never leave you."

The fields are white for the harvest is great and ripe, and it is ready for the gospel sickle; oh, where are the laborers to gather the golden grain into the Master's garner?

My dear sister in Christ, may the Spirit of God come upon you, and make you willing to do the work the Lord has assigned to you, and cause your light to shine!

—*Maria Woodworth-Etter*
1916

Father, anoint me to use all my talents, gifts, and abilities to bring You glory. Teach me to use them wisely so that I may be a shining light for You. Amen.

"Women's Right in the Gospel," *Signs and Wonders.*

Day 5
Remember You Are Loved

READ JOHN 3:16

It is vital that you as a woman realize that God paid a supreme price for you—the blood and life of His only begotten Son, Jesus Christ. He would never pay such a price for a *nobody*. He would only pay such a price for a *somebody*. You are God's prize! You are valuable to God's divine plan.

You may have lived sinfully. But remember that Jesus Christ only saves sinners. God's pardon is only for those who have done wrong. God's redemption is only for those who are lost. His salvation is only for people who are not what they could have been.

So embrace God's opinion of yourself, and you will no longer want to destroy the wonderful person that God made in you. You will value your body, your mind, your lungs, your organs, your blood, your heart. Since He accepts you, you can accept yourself, and you will begin to accept others.

And always . . . always . . . remember you are loved.

—*Daisy Washburn Osborn*
1991

Father, I praise You for loving me and for teaching me to love, respect, and accept myself. Because You love me, I can now love myself and others too. Amen.

Women and Self-Esteem, (Tulsa, OK: OSFO Publishers, 1991).

Weekend
Wait on God

READ JAMES 5:13–18

Never be afraid to be quiet before God. Never be afraid to wait on the Lord. We can well afford to wait on the Lord. Isn't it beautiful when He stills all this human thing, and He gets through to us? He has to quiet that human thing in us that's just up racing and ranting all the time. That's one of the reasons why so many of our prayers aren't answered and we don't get from God what we would like to have.

I was so glad to see a man who wanted the baptism of the Holy Ghost finally pray, "O God, won't You please take the hurry-up out of me?" Well, before the meeting was over, God was able to take the hurry-up out of him, and he got the baptism in the Holy Spirit once he waited on God.

—*Hattie Hammond*
n.d.

O God, won't You please take the hurry-up out of me?
Help me to wait on You and to receive all that You
have for me, in Christ. Amen.

Audiocassette titled "How to Pray," from a chapel service at Christ for the Nations.

Week 3—Day 1

Something Happened

READ ACTS 1:8; 2:1–39

My very first association with the Holy Spirit was in a little Methodist church in Concordia, Missouri, one Sunday morning while sitting with Mama in church. It was time for the last song to be sung, but just then something happened to me. I do not remember one word the preacher said. All I remember is that at that moment I began to shake and tremble.

At that moment I saw myself for what I was—a sinner in the sight of God. I stood there in the front pew and wept, and at that moment I was born again. It was the new birth experience, and I have never doubted being saved since. Never!

I believe that when you are born again there is a definite time and place—and you will know it! The Holy Spirit will bear witness with your spirit as your spirit passes from death to life. It's been the new birth experience that has been so real to me, from that first moment I had contact with the Holy Spirit.

—*Kathryn Kuhlman*
n.d.

Heavenly Father, fill us with the Holy Spirit so that we know beyond any shadow of doubt that we have been born again and that Your Spirit fills us and empowers us to do great exploits in Your name. Amen.

Audiocassette titled "My First Experience With the Holy Spirit," from a chapel service at Oral Roberts University.

Day 2

"Preach Holiness!"

READ 2 CORINTHIANS 7:1; HEBREWS 12:10

One morning as I awoke, I heard the Holy Spirit say, "Hattie, My child, preach holiness!" He brought to my remembrance a woman who asked me to meet her at the throne of grace. "Pardon me," she exclaimed as she noticed those kneeling at the altar and crying out for God to cleanse them. "Is this the way you have to go?"

"Yes," I answered. "And it's a blessed way!"

"Oh, it's a hard way!" she replied.

What way? First to the cross, then to the throne, by the cleansing blood of Jesus! It is the message of holiness, and it is a straight, narrow way. The next morning she came to church and said, "I have spent the previous day straightening up old accounts—but I have nowhere begun to straighten all that has to be straightened!" A change could indeed be plainly seen in her face.

After seeing such a miracle of transformation in even one life my heart was readily moved to say, "O God, by Thy grace I want to—and will—preach holiness!"

—*Hattie Hammond*
January 1928

> *Father, we thank You for the gift of sanctification.*
> *Help us to lead holy lives before You that our lights*
> *may testify of Your power to transform us from sinners*
> *to saints. Amen.*

From her diary.

Day 3
Fleas!

READ 1 THESSALONIANS

"Fleas!" I cried. "Betsie, the place is swarming with them! . . . Betsie, how can we live in such a place?"

The "place" was Ravensbruck.

"Corrie!" she said excitedly. "He's given us the answer! Before we asked, as He always does! In the Bible this morning . . . Where was it? Read that part again!"

I glanced down the long dim aisle to make sure no guard was in sight, then drew the Bible from its pouch. "It was in First Thessalonians," I said. We were on our third complete reading of the New Testament since leaving Scheveningen. In the feeble light I turned the pages. "Here it is: 'Comfort the frightened, help the weak, be patient with everyone. See that none of you repays evil for evil, but always seek to do good to one another and to all. . . .'"

"Go on," said Betsie. "That wasn't all!"

"Oh yes—'Rejoice always, pray constantly, give thanks in all circumstances; for this is the will of God in Christ Jesus.'"

"That's it, Corrie! That's His answer. 'Give thanks in all circumstances!' That's what we can do. We can start right now to thank God for every single thing about this new barracks!"

I stared at her, then around me in the dark, foul-aired room.

"Such as?" I said.

"Such as being assigned here together."

I bit my lip. "Oh yes, Lord Jesus!"

"Such as what you're holding in your hands."

I looked down at the Bible. "Yes! Thank You, dear Lord,

that there was no inspection when we entered here! Thank You for all the women here in this room who will meet You in these pages."

"Yes," said Betsie. "Thank You for the very crowding here. Since we're packed in so close, that many more will hear!" She looked at me expectantly. "Corrie!" she prodded.

"Oh, all right. Thank You for the jammed, crammed, stuffed, packed, suffocating crowds."

"Thank You," Betsie went on serenely, "for the fleas . . . "

—Corrie ten Boom
1971

> *Lord, help us to be thankful and to praise You always, in each and every circumstance—even the painful, hard places in life. We glorify You, Lord, even for the small, annoying things—the "fleas" You use to shape and polish us as gems for Your glorious crown. Amen!*

The Hiding Place, (Minneapolis, MN: World Wide Publications, 1971).

Day 4

Hastening the Day

READ 2 PETER 3:12

In the past, I was known as a preacher who preached the baptism of the Holy Spirit and the Second Coming of the Lord. In those days, when I preached the return of Jesus Christ, I expected it to happen the very next minute. I thought He would come right then, but He didn't. When this thing happened, I thought He'd come; when that thing happened, I thought He'd come. But He didn't. When Israel was made a nation, I said, "This is it!" But Israel has been a nation for a good many years now, and still He hasn't come.

So what is He waiting for? And why is He waiting while the world is getting worse and worse?

It's simply this: The church has not made herself ready quite yet. He is waiting for her to do it.

The church—which is His body—has everything to do with how soon He comes back. He is coming as quickly as He has something ready to come for. We—the Bride—must make ourselves ready before He will come back for us. That is what will hasten the day of His return.

—*Clara Grace*
April 1967

Lord, make us ready for You! Dress us in fine raiment; cleanse us from all sin. Make us pure, without spot or wrinkle, and hasten the glorious day of Your return! Amen!

"Hastening the Day of the Lord," from a service in Tulsa, Oklahoma.

Day 5

Recipe for Revival

READ 2 CHRONICLES 7:13–14; JOEL 2–3

The prophet Joel called for the people to fast. This was not just a call to prayer, but to pray and fast, and for the ministers to weep between the porch and the altar. (See Joel 2:17.) No church is going to see revival unless the ministers get down on their faces with the people and admit that they are bankrupt . . . until they admit that they are powerless and haven't got what they are professing to have. That is the recipe for revival.

God cannot help anyone until each person comes to the end of himself. He can't help until people come to the end of their sermon-making and to the end of playing church.

When we come to the end of ourselves, then God can move! If we do this, then God says He will leave us a blessing behind. As the prophet Joel wrote, God has promised that He will pour out His Spirit and that His sons and His daughters would prophesy. The latter-day rain! Revival!

— *Myrtle D. Beall*
1950

Lord, give me the determination to pray and fast that Your Spirit might be poured out upon my life—and through my life—to others. Amen.

"Recipe for Revival," from a wire recording from a radio program.

Weekend

The Power of Repentance

READ MATTHEW 21:28–29; 2 CORINTHIANS 7:9–11

*W*hat is true repentance? The Greek word *repentance* means "to have another mind," or "to change the mind." It is used in the New Testament to indicate a change of mind concerning sin, God, and self. This change of mind may be preceded by sorrow, but sorrow for sin, though it may "work" repentance, is *not* repentance.

Repentance is not a voluntary feeling of any kind. It is turning away from disobedience to obedience. It is willing and feeling as God does concerning sin, and always implies forsaking sin.

Because you are a free moral agent you have the power, but you have no right, to keep yourself from under God's control. God says, "Ye are not your own, for ye are bought with a price: therefore glorify God in your body, and in your spirit, which are God's" 1 Cor. 6:19–20). Jesus said, "There is joy in the presence of the angels of God over one sinner that repenteth" Luke 15:10).

—*Mrs. F. F. Bosworth*
n.d.

Lord, I repent. I have been purchased by the blood of Your sacrifice on Calvary. I turn away from sin and forsake it forever. Amen.

From a tract titled *The "Why?" and "How?" of Salvation*.

Week 4—Day 1
Stay Prayed Up!

READ LUKE 11:1; ACTS 6:4; 1 THESSALONIANS 5:17

Stay prayed up. The only way you can stay prayed up is to pray through every day. When you pray, determine that you will pray until you pray through!

If you are in turmoil and need peace, then speak peace to your troubled heart and all that is not right there—all that barrenness and dryness. Hate it! Hate it with everything that is in you! Hate every moment that you are away from the Lord and out of His presence! Press in and pray through. And when you get hold of Him, never let Him go.

Will you pray through with me?

—Hattie Hammond
n.d.

Father, wash us clean. Forgive us for every sin that we have committed, right up to this present moment. Forgive our prayerlessness. Forgive our dryness. Forgive our lethargy. Forgive us for giving in to our flesh and becoming lazy. Forgive us for procrastinating. Forgive us for turning to others instead of turning to You. Forgive us for wasting our time with magazines and other distractions instead of feeding on the Living Bread. Forgive us! We repent of our sins before You. Help us, Father, to pray through—and stay prayed up! In Jesus' name we pray. Amen.

"How to Pray," from a chapel service at Christ for the Nations.

Day 2
The Prayer of Faith

READ JAMES 5:14–15; EPHESIANS 6:18

We read in James, chapter 5, that "the prayer of faith shall save the sick." Yet when our friends and neighbors are sick, they remain sick for months and years, and the arm of the flesh proves too short to help them. We do not think of applying to "the Great Physician" with faith in His power to heal.

In James, we read that God will raise up the sick, "and if he have committed sins they shall be forgiven him" (5:15). Who is it that has the power to forgive sins?

"God," you answer.

When the Lord impresses upon the mind of one of His suffering children that "the prayer of faith shall save the sick," and when He leads one of His faithful followers who is "holding fast the profession of his faith" to follow out the command in James, chapter 5, to anoint the sick with oil in the name of the Lord and to offer up the prayer of faith, then God shall answer. Then He shall raise up the sick one, to His glory and praise!

—*Mrs. Edward Mix*
n.d.

Lord, increase my faith so that I may hold fast to the profession of my faith when standing for the healing of myself and others. In Jesus' name. Amen.

"Holding Fast," *Triumphs of Faith.*

Day 3

Claiming the Promise

READ LUKE 10:19; ACTS 1:8; 2 TIMOTHY 1:7

At a recent meeting, after the altar call Sister Etter had been praying for many 'round the altar and God wonderfully healed them all. As she was praying for a lady, Sister Etter noticed there was a scorpion laying two inches from her hand. She reached to knock it off, and it stung her. The pain, she said, seemed to run all through her and go to her heart. Her finger turned red, and the Lord showed her that it was a fatal and poisonous sting. Nothing but the Lord could help her.

A brother standing nearby killed the scorpion, and several of the saints who saw what had happened went right to praying. Sister Etter claimed the promise that we should have power over serpents and scorpions, and all fear left her Luke 10:19).

She hung on to the Lord, and His promises, and the pain stopped. She went right on praying for the sick, and nothing was left but the mark of the sting.

—*Carrie Judd Montgomery*
1925

Lord, I claim that same promise! In Jesus' name. Amen.

Life and Testimony: Biography of Mrs. M. B. Woodworth-Etter, (Indianapolis, IN: August Fieck, 1925).

Day 4

Miracle-Working Faith

READ JOHN 2:3; ACTS 19:11; 1 CORINTHIANS 12:10

The centurion had great faith—so much that he did not need Jesus to be present in order to speak a word that would heal his ailing servant. Surprised at such faith, Jesus healed the servant.

You can never have faith without meeting His conditions. When you meet the conditions of surrender and obedience, He will drop faith right down into your heart; it is the gift of God.

Jesus will not do anything today without faith. You must not only have faith in God, but you must have the very faith of Jesus Christ—the faith that Jesus Himself had. When God said a thing to Jesus, He knew that God was going to do it. And that is the faith He will give to you today—miracle-working faith!

—Mrs. M. B. Woodworth-Etter
January 1916

Lord, give me that same faith as Jesus—miracle-working faith, faith that makes something happen! Take all doubt from me and cause me to expect the miraculous move of God in answer to my prayers. Thank You for the gift of faith. Amen.

Triumphs of Faith.

Day 5

Hungering After God

READ JOB 19:25; MATTHEW 5:6

O dear heart, if you have hunger, cherish and encourage that hunger as you would your life. It is put there by the Holy Spirit to lead you closer to God.

When I hear someone telling what a great person he is and how good he lives, I think, *Poor soul! He is so far from God!* I have learned that the nearer we get to Jesus, the smaller and more imperfect our own self life appears in our eyes. He grows bigger and more perfect and lovely at each onward step until, in the light of His righteousness, we fall prostrate at His feet and cry with Job, "I have heard of thee by the hearing of the ear; but now mine eye seeth thee: wherefore I abhor myself, and repent in dust and ashes" (Job 42:5).

After coming to the end of self-righteousness, an all-absorbing, unquenchable hunger engulfs us. He will give us beauty for ashes, rejoicing for mourning, victory for defeat, His righteousness for our unrighteousness. Blessed are they that hunger; they shall be filled.

—*Aimee Semple McPherson*
n.d.

Fill me, Lord, with unquenchable hunger for the things of the Spirit, so that as You increase Your work in me, I will decrease. Bring me to the end of my self-righteousness that I may walk in the righteousness of Christ. Amen!

Triumphs of Faith. Used by permission of the Heritage Department of the Foursquare Gospel.

Weekend

Walk in Love

READ EPHESIANS 5:1–2; PHILIPPIANS 4:8

If I do things because I want my own way, or to please myself, or because I think it is right, I do not love God or people but I love myself. To live the love life, self must never be considered or humored. If I speak one word that is not filled with love, whether it is what I know or what I have heard, even if all is true—I am not walking in love. This world is full of evil, and I must constantly come into contact with it, but God says I am to put away an evil thing as soon as I see it and refuse to remember it. As soon as I hear an evil thing, I am to put it away—forget it. And the only way I can do these things is to stay my mind on God—what He is—and on His Word.

God says, "Love covereth all sins." If I walk in love, no matter what sin I see in others, I must quickly cover it over with love and positively refuse to see it, think of it, or remember anything except what is good. That is walking in love!

—*Mrs. C. Nuzum*
June 1938

Lord, help me to walk in love because it does not come easily for me to put aside myself. Help me to fix my eyes on You—and forget all that I see and hear around me except for the good, except for Your Word, until love covers all. Amen.

Triumphs of Faith.

Week 5—Day 1
Living in Tents

READ 2 TIMOTHY 2:1–13

In summer and in winter, north or south, I worked by day and dreamed by night in the shadow of a tent. I slept on a soldier's canvas cot in a little tent beside the big one, myself and my two children; and as I slept, I sometimes stroked the sides of the cot and thought that I, too, was a soldier, bivouacked upon the battleground of the Lord.

We traveled thousands of miles, from hamlet to town and from town to city, and thousands of souls found the golden stairs within canvas walls as my tents and I went up and down the land, seeking those whose need was greater.

Sometimes, when the wind howled and the sleet came slanting-wise in sheets, I would have to stay up from dusk to dawn with a sledgehammer in my hand, driving in stakes as fast as they were loosened in the ground; and sometimes, after a meeting, I would sit staring into the heart of a dying campfire, alone under the stars with the palm fronds whispering their lullaby, seeking to read in the glow of the embers a message for the morrow.

—*Aimee Semple McPherson*
1927

> *Heavenly Father, don't ever let me forget that I'm a soldier in Your army. Help me to prepare myself to stand fast as the storms hit, and to always be ready to endure whatever hardships come. Amen.*

"Where's There's a Will...," *In Service of the King* (New York: Boni and Liveright, 1927). Used by permission of the Heritage Department of the Foursquare Gospel.

Day 2
No Limits

READ MATTHEW 27:55–61; MARK 16:1–10; LUKE 8:1–3

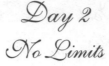God never planned for any woman to become a non-achiever or a failure in life. No woman was ever intended for prostitution or infidelity, for neglect or shame, for sickness or suffering, for destructiveness or nonproductivity. No woman was ever destined by God to crawl in shame or to cower in a subservient role.

Mary Magdalene was a vivid example. Jesus saw in her the strength of her resolve to believe in Him, even when the men retreated in seclusion after His crucifixion. They were afraid and were filled with unbelief. But Christ saw Mary's qualities. Others saw her past problems and her record as a demon-possessed woman. No wonder it amazed the disciples when Mary Magdalene was the one who brought them the news that Christ had risen and that she had seen the Lord. . . .

There are no limits for a woman who follows Christ.

—*Daisy Washburn Osborn*
1990

Father, thank You that You see my potential, not my past. Help me to see myself in the light of that potential—and to realize that in Christ there are no limits. In Jesus' name. Amen.

New Life for Women (Tulsa, OK: OSFO Publishers, 1991).

Day 3

A Woman Ahead of Her Time

READ ACTS 5:27–39

Saved when she was twelve years old, Maria Woodworth-Etter heard the voice of Jesus saying, "Go out and gather lost sheep." But in the late 1800s the church did not allow women to preach the gospel. So Maria told the Lord, "When I grow up, I'll marry a missionary [the church allowed women to do that]; then I'll serve You."

But God's plan for Maria was not limited by the religious dogmas of her day. He never gave up on His dream for her, and Maria finally said, "Yes."

That remarkable woman preached the gospel until she was eighty years old, despite incredible opposition. And that was before the epoch of political rhetoric about the constitutional rights of women. The church and the public had no tolerance for a woman preacher.

But Maria succeeded in becoming what God wanted her to be. She exercised her choice of power. She chose to obey God instead of man or culture or tradition.

—*Daisy Washburn Osborn*
1990

> *Lord, I exercise my power of choice today as I decide to obey You and disregard every seeming obstacle. Through Christ, I shall overcome every hindrance to my reaching my full potential and fulfilling to the letter Your call on my life. Amen!*

The Woman Believer (Tulsa, OK: OSFO Publishers, 1990).

Day 4
Clear Leadings

READ PSALM 119:30–44

I was not always able to get clear leadings from the Lord. In my agonizing to hear Him, I would get in such a tumult inside that God could not talk to me. I had to get perfectly calm and quiet in my spirit.

We desire God's best, but something stands in the way that we are not able to surrender because it hurts to give it up. It's some sore spot that we don't want people to talk about or put their finger on; every time anyone touches it, we cringe. We are happy as long as we can keep it covered, but when the Holy Spirit begins to probe, we cringe and wriggle, twist and groan. But there is only one way to get relief: Lean back and let Him probe until He gets to the bottom. When the sore is taken out by the Holy Spirit, the spot cleansed by the blood of Jesus, there is great relief.

Today it is our privilege to get so close to God, so still that when He speaks we can hear His slightest whisper. If we—like John the beloved—are close enough to lean upon His breast, we must hear Him speak. Then we'll have clear leadings.

—*Mrs. Lydia Markley Piper*
April 1909

> *Lord, help me to get still enough to hear Your voice,*
> *calm enough to remain quiet as You remove the spots.*
> *Give me clear leadings, Lord! Amen.*

The Latter Rain Evangel.

Day 5
Water, Fire, Wind

READ ISAIAH 44:1–5; ACTS 2

The Holy Ghost is likened to three elements—water, fire, and wind—three of the most destructive forces in the universe, and three of the most useful. In all their force, these elements give us an idea of the mighty power of the Holy Ghost.

He is called "water." The Lord promised, "I will pour water on him that is thirsty, and floods upon the dry ground." A tidal wave of glory is coming this way.

He is called "fire." Such fire provides light and warmth and, to the Christian, both burns away the dross and sparks the passion necessary to lead a dying world to life eternal.

As "wind," the Holy Ghost—with gales as great as any cyclone—strikes people as the great leveler. In its wake are swept away all thought of money bags and materialism, hatred and ill-will. The cyclone of God's power sweeps out all that encumbers us.

—*Maria Woodworth-Etter*
July 1913

Thank You, Lord, for the force of the Holy Spirit—water when I'm dry and thirsty; fire when I need its burning; wind to blow away the hindrances. Thank You, Lord, that all three aspects of the Holy Spirit's power are for my good and Your glory. Amen.

Weekend

Abandonment to God

READ PSALM 23

The activity of the natural selfish life is the greatest obstacle to your progress. Applaud not yourself when you have done well. Admit no reflection in regard to the good you have accomplished, so that all that nourishes self-complacency may die.

Possess your soul in peace as much as possible; not by effort, but by ceasing from effort; by letting go everything that troubles you. Be quiet, that you may settle, as we leave water to settle when agitated. When you discover your errors and sins, do not stop under whatever good pretext to remedy them. Rather, abandon yourself at once to God, that He may destroy in you all that is displeasing to Him. I assure you, you are not capable of yourself to correct the least fault. Your only remedy is abandonment to God and remaining quiet in His hands. If you discovered the depth of inward corruption in your heart, your courage would fail!

Rest assured, God loves you. Have faith in His love and mercy. You will see farther by and by. . . .

—*Madame Jeanne Marie Guyon*
1935

> *Lord, help me to keep my eyes so fixed on You that I look neither to the right nor to the left—not to my own accomplishments, not to the past, not to those things You have wrought through me. In Jesus' name. Amen.*

"Abandonment to God," *Spiritual Letters* (Milwaukee, WI: n.p., 1935).

Week 6—Day 1
Skimpy Faith

READ MATTHEW 17:20; 21:21–22

Someone has said that a little faith takes us to heaven . . . but a whole lot of faith (much faith) will bring heaven to us, right here on earth. We can't have heaven on earth with skimpy faith.

Skimpy faith makes me think of the walk in front of the parsonage in Newman, Georgia, made of cement slabs—one here, one there. The whole thing looks rather like a hit-and-miss job—a lovely parsonage, but a skimpy walk. I don't think I ever passed over this walk, but that I wondered why anyone would leave so much out, and put so little in. It was so hard to walk in that manner— a hit-and-miss attitude, a little here, a little there.

I am sure there was plenty of cement. Perhaps there was little with which to buy it. The same is true with God: There is plenty of power, but little faith, which is the only thing that will bring in the power of God. It seems a shame such faith should be so skimpy, especially since God has made provision for us to have the solid pavement of faith in His promises at all times.

—*Mildred Wicks*
n.d.

Lord, please don't let it be said of me that my faith was "skimpy faith." Increase my faith so that I may apprehend the power of the Holy Spirit. Amen.

The Dawn of a Better Day (Tulsa, OK: Standard Publishing).

Day 2
Put Out Your Tongue

READ PSALM 34:12–13; PROVERBS 12:18; 18:21

When I was a child I was filled with misgivings each time my mother lined me up in front of a doctor, for the first thing he said to me was, "Put out your tongue!" And when I put out my poor, little, trembling tongue, he would make an awful frown, "This child has been eating trash. Give her no supper and put her early to bed." Worse, he would say, "Give her a dose of castor oil!" I used to think, *How wise he must be! How can he possibly tell what's wrong with me just by looking at my tongue?*

When I got older and became a doctor myself, I would say to my patients, "Put out your tongue!" I had learned that a clean, pink tongue was the very index of health; and that a swollen, discolored, furry tongue was a sure indication that there was something seriously wrong.

Then I found the Great Physician and commenced to study His Book. My expansive medical library was reduced to just one volume. In it, I found a remedy for every ailment, spiritual and physical, to which flesh is heir.

When we say yes to Jesus, we must put out our tongues—examine ourselves to see what it is that is in our hearts, for it shall surely come to our tongues.

—*Dr. Lillian Yeomans*
May 1926

Father, help me to train my tongue so that only words that uplift others, edify me, and glorify You will be spoken. In Jesus' name. Amen.

The Latter Rain Evangel.

Day 3

Words of a Talebearer

READ PROVERBS 18:8;19:9

Talebearing is one of the most dangerous occupations anybody can engage in. I believe that some of the diseases affecting the deepest tissues of the body are due to a misuse of our tongues.

The first such instance I can think of is Miriam who was stricken with leprosy because of the misuse of her tongue. She spoke against Moses because he married an Ethiopian woman. Only when Moses prayed for his sister was she healed.

In order to have clean, healthy tongues, we must also have pure hearts, for "out of the abundance of the heart the mouth speaketh." God wants our lives absolutely yielded to Him so that the Holy Ghost can take possession of our tongues and praise Jesus in a language we have never known—a heavenly language.

This tongue that has so often been a source of evil is capable of uttering the highest and holiest aspirations of the human heart.

—*Dr. Lillian Yeomans*
July 1926

Lord, sanctify my tongue but purify my heart also. Thank You for revealing to me the divine connection between the contents of my heart and the words I speak. Amen.

The Latter Rain Evangel.

Day 4
Eagles

READ DEUTERONOMY 32:11–12; ISAIAH 40:31

The eagle builds her nest of thorns and lines it with down. Inside the tiny eaglets are tenderly cared for.

Eagles were meant to mount above the storm clouds. So to get the eaglets to fly, the mother pulls out the down from the sides of the nest—much to the dismay of the little eaglets who climb upon the edge of the nest to get away from those ugly thorns. With a little blow she pushes the eaglets off their perch and they go tumbling and shrieking through the air. Again and again they are pushed off into thin air . . . until they lose their fear. A new joy takes possession of them, along with new life and power as they mount the heavens and soar away.

So it is with humans. How the human heart loves to build its little nest and gather around it the persons and things that please it most and settle down. But our heavenly Father loves us too well; sooner or later He begins to stir up the nest. "As an eagle stirreth up her nest, fluttereth over her young, spreadeth abroad her wings, taketh them, beareth them on her wings; so the Lord alone did lead him" (Deut. 32:11–12). Thorns are often greater blessings than the down.

—*Miss Alice B. Garrigus*
March 1926

> *Lord, help me both to understand and endure the thorns that are necessary to prod me to fly higher. In Jesus' name. Amen.*

Day 5
"If It Be Thy Will..."

READ MATTHEW 12:50; ROMANS 12:1–2

When the Lord says, "Come unto me all ye that labor and are heavy laden," we don't say, "Lord, I will come unto Thee if it be Thy will," but, "I come because Thou sayest it is Thy will." Equally we can say, "Lord, I seek for healing because Thou has commanded me to do so; I do it because it is Thy will."

It is "the prayer of faith" that saves the sick, and none can pray the prayer of faith unless they are sure about the will of God. "This is the confidence that we have in him, that, if we ask anything according to his will, he heareth us: and if we know that he hear us, whatsoever we ask, we know that we have the petitions that we desired of him" (1 John 5:14–15). The prayer of faith admits no doubt, for where doubt is, there faith is not.

—Mrs. M. Baxter
July 1884

Thank You, Lord, for the gift of faith. Thank You that by faith I can come to You and make my petitions known. Thank You that You hear me, and You will grant my petitions. In Jesus' name. Amen.

The Latter Rain Evangel.

Weekend

First-Class Women

READ ESTHER 4:13–15; LUKE 2:36–38

In the church and in God's program, He never designed women to be second-class members with limited expression. Religious traditions and customs have been relentless in their suppression of the female part of the body of Christ. Those extraordinary women who have overcome feminine subjugation and have dared to do exploits in Christ's name have had little recorded about their triumphs of faith.

Even in politics, it has only been a few years since women gained the right to vote in most of the industrialized world.

God has a beautiful plan for you that no one else on earth can fulfill, because you are unique. You are the only one of you that God has.

Women are created to be first-class persons.

—Daisy Washburn Osborn
1990

> *Lord, help me to always remember that You created me to be unique, and that You have a beautiful plan for my life. Thank You that You created me to be a first-class person. In Jesus' name. Amen.*

Women Without Limits, (Tulsa, OK: OSFO Publishers, 1990).

Week 7—Day 1
God's Gift of Forgiveness

READ ROMANS 5:12–21; 1 JOHN 1:9; ISAIAH 53:6

In God's plan of forgiveness, Christ was wounded for your transgressions. He was bruised for your iniquities. The chastisement (or the punishment that you deserved because of your sin) was laid upon Him, and by His stripes you were healed. (Or, since He endured your punishment, you as a woman are forgiven—restored to God, and healed of your estrangement from God, with its consequences, if you know about it and believe it.)

Your sins are already judged and punished in Christ. He already assumed your penalty in your place. He did it so that you would be absolved from all guilt, condemnation, and judgment.

Since a crime cannot be punished twice, or can a debt be paid twice, you and I are liberated through forgiveness. In order to accept God's forgiveness, you need to know about it. "Faith comes by hearing" (or by knowing) God's Word (God's plan of forgiveness).

—*Daisy Washburn Osborn*
1990

Lord, help me to know Your Word as it pertains to the forgiveness of sins. Help me to walk in the fullness of the liberation that Your forgiveness provides. In Jesus' name. Amen.

Women Without Limits, (Tulsa, OK: OSFO Publishers, 1990).

Day 2

Righteousness

READ EPHESIANS 2:8–10; PHILIPPIANS 3:8–11

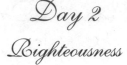Without the knowledge of the Good News, we search instinctively to find peace with God. Through good works, through philosophy, through religion, or through other means, we search. We may try church attendance, benevolence, penance, prayers, fastings, confessions, abstention from pleasures and from bad habits, self-denial, pilgrimages, even laceration and punishment of our own bodies in the insatiable quest for spiritual satisfaction.

Yet the tormenting consciousness of sin, of guilt, and of unworthiness before God persists as long as you remain uninformed about God's plan of forgiveness and salvation. Christ gave His life to bear the penalty of every sin that you ever committed. You can actually receive God's forgiveness and His righteousness now—just by accepting it in your heart. Then you will be a woman who can stand in God's presence without the sense of fear, of guilt, or of inferiority. That is what we call righteousness—or right standing—before God.

—Daisy Washburn Osborn
1990

Father, I accept Your love for me, and Your forgiveness.
Help me to walk in love and forgiveness toward myself
and others. In Jesus' name. Amen.

Women Without Limits, (Tulsa, OK: OSFO Publishers, 1990).

Day 3

The Marys and the Marthas

READ NUMBERS 11:29; JOHN 4:10–29, 39–42

God is calling the Marys and the Marthas today all over our land to work in various places in the vineyard of the Lord. God grant that they may respond and say, "Lord, here am I; send me." This call was made after Christ had risen. Again in the New Testament are the words of the prophet Joel echoed: "I will pour out in the last days of my spirit." These words refer in a special manner to these last days. God is promising great blessings and power to His handmaidens for the last great harvest just before the notable Day of the Lord.

We must first be baptized into Christ by the one Spirit—that is, to be born of the Spirit. Then we ought to be anointed with power and wisdom. The Spirit ought to be poured out like oil on our heads, to give us knowledge of the deep things of God. The Lord also says we shall prophesy. Paul says, "Desire spiritual gifts, but rather that ye may prophesy" (1 Cor. 14:1). The Lord has promised this greatest gift to His handmaidens and daughters.

—*Maria Woodworth-Etter*
1916

> *Lord, here am I; send me! I want to be used by You during this End-Time harvest of souls. Make me a Mary or a Martha in Your service. In Jesus' name, I pray. Amen.*

M. B. Woodworth-Etter, *Signs and Wonders* (Bartlesville, OK: Oak Tree Publications, Inc., 1916).

Day 4
The Last Call

READ 1 THESSALONIANS 4:13–18; JAMES 5:7–8

The Lord of Hosts is with us today, for a crown of glory, and a diadem of beauty unto the residue of His people, and with great power to those that press the battle to the gates.

He is giving His wisdom to the weak, to those who naturally have not the wisdom of this world. He is teaching knowledge and making us to understand. Those who are weaned from the milk; little children, and those who are not learned; and revealing and manifesting Himself to them. Yea, He reveals the deep things of God, speaking in new tongues as the Spirit gives utterance, showing the wonderful work of God. With stammering lips and other tongues He speaks to His people, yet for all that some will not believe. It is a special sign that Jesus is coming soon. See 1 Thessalonians 4:16.)

Be careful how you hear and act. It is the last call. We will not be surprised at anything our God does.

—*Maria Woodworth-Etter*
1916

Lord, help me to understand the times we live in, and to walk carefully. Help me to embrace the work of the Holy Spirit, for I realize that this is the last call. Guide me to Scripture verses that will further instruct me about what to expect during Your outpouring. In Jesus' name. Amen.

M. B. Woodworth-Etter, *Signs and Wonders* (Bartlesville, OK: Oak Tree Publications, Inc., 1916).

Day 5

Going to the Upper Room

READ ACTS 2

What a procession they must have made, that little hundred and twenty!

Yonder goes Mary Magdalene. From another direction come James and John. There are Andrew and Phillip, Bartholomew and Matthew . . . and round the corner comes Mary, the mother of Jesus. Though her head is bent a little and the lines of her pale face reveal the suffering and the sword that has lately pierced her heart, there is a new light—a glorious hope—shining in her eyes.

"And suddenly there came a sound from heaven as of a rushing mighty wind, and it filled all the house where they were sitting. And there appeared unto them cloven tongues like as of fire, and it sat upon each of them. And they were all filled with the Holy Ghost, and began to speak in other tongues, as the Spirit gave them utterance" (Acts 2:2–4).

The Lord had kept His Word—the Comforter had come.

—*Aimee Semple McPherson*
November 1919

Thank You, Lord, for the Comforter, and for all the gifts contained in Him. Thank You for the infilling of the Holy Spirit, and for the finished work of Christ at Calvary. Help me to walk in the fullness of the Holy Spirit and the finished work of Christ. In Jesus' name. Amen.

The Pentecostal Evangel. Used by permission of the Heritage Department of the Foursquare Gospel.

Weekend

Power From on High

READ ACTS 1:4; ROMANS 8:24–28

In that Upper Room were those who had failed in the past. There were those who had doubted and denied. Have you failed in the past? Have you at times denied your Lord just when you should have stood most true? Have you been a doubting Thomas? And do you feel your need of strength and power?

Believer, have you been used mightily in the past in soulwinning? Have the sick been healed and demons cast out in answer to your prayers? If so, thank God, but you too—like Peter and John, Mary and Martha, Mary the mother of Jesus, Thomas and Bartholomew—need the Holy Spirit. Oh, how you need Him!

Jesus is coming soon. That message must be broadcast, and souls gathered in before His appearing. He has called you to go. Preach the gospel! Witness to all those about you. Go—but tarry until the Holy Spirit has come in to abide, and until you have been endued with power from on high.

—*Aimee Semple McPherson*
1916

Lord, fill me with Your power from on high. As I wait before You in prayer, empower me with those spiritual gifts that will help me to take Your message of hope, love, salvation, and forgiveness to a lost and dying world. In Jesus' name. Amen.

The Pentecostal Evangel. Used by permission of the Heritage Department of the Foursquare Gospel.

Week 8—Day 1
The Way to Perdition?

READ TITUS 3:3–7; 1 JOHN 4:8–12

One evening my voice was weary from long strain. A young Christian gentleman said: "Sister, give me the megaphone, and I will shout out an invitation."

Rather dubiously I surrendered the megaphone.

Just then, a man rounded the corner. Aiming the megaphone at him, my friend—to my horror—cried out: "Say, Brother! Do you know that you are on your way to perdition?"

I seized the megaphone and called to the driver, "Go on! Go on, quickly!"

That poor astounded man on the street! As soon as we had rounded a corner, I said to my megaphone friend, "Why, Brother—*why* did you do that?"

"Well, he *was* on his way, wasn't he?"

"*But how do you know?*" I responded. "And even if he were, that is not the way to win souls to Christ! One can do more with the bait of love than with the club of bombastic preaching."

—*Aimee Semple McPherson*
1927

Lord, help me to reach the lost with the bait of love,
and leave my "megaphone" at home! In Jesus' name.
Amen.

In the Service of the King (Foursquare Publications, 1988, originally written 1927). Used by permission of the Heritage Department of the Foursquare Gospel.

Day 2
Two Kinds of Giving

READ MARK 10:29–30; 2 CORINTHIANS 9:6–8

Some time ago a minister—whose only child, a daughter, was called to go to China—felt as though he could scarcely bear it. At last the beautiful daughter left for China. The next day a friend who went to visit found the father smiling and happy. "What has happened?" the visitor asked.

The minister replied. "When I went down to the big ocean liner this morning to see my daughter set sail, a man came along. Both of us stood watching the boat go out. 'Brother,' I asked, 'whom have you on that boat that is going to China?' 'Why,' he replied. 'I have just given a hundred thousand dollars to send the missionaries over there—and it's all on that boat!'

"I said, 'I have given my daughter—that little lamb that I loved so. She is going to China.'

"'Oh,' said the other man. 'I thought I had given something, but sir, my hundred thousand dollars is not as much as your daughter's little finger. It is *you* who have given all.'"

Oh, if we want to be soul-winners, we must be willing to give our all to Jesus!

—Aimee Semple McPherson
November 1923

Father, I surrender all to You—body, soul, and spirit. Use me as You will. Amen.

"Two Men Who Gave," *This Is That.* Used by permission of the Heritage Department of the Foursquare Gospel.

Day 3
Worse Than Judas

READ MATTHEW 26:15; 27:3–9

Many sell their Savior at a lesser price than Judas did. He obtained thirty pieces of silver, but I have known some, who from indulgence in a wrong habit or the retainment of an injurious friend; others for some trifling adornments, with many other foolish and hurtful lusts, which might seem so small that the very mention of them would cause a blush of shame. Should you ask such a one, "Do you think that object worth thirty pieces of silver?" the answer would be frankly returned, "No!" These do not mean to part with the Savior for such trifles—but the matter ends in this, and they do in reality part with the Savior as effectually as though there had been a formal bargain, as in the case of Judas Iscariot.

A variety of instances in which the Savior has been kept out of the heart come up before the vision of my mind. There must be a reason why the Lord has not revealed Himself fully to you. Perhaps there is something on your mind that you think you may have to do after you get religion, which you are not willing to do now.

—*Phoebe Palmer*
1855

Lord, forgive me for putting things large and small ahead of You, and thereby sacrificing relationship with You! I repent, and gladly give up whatever is in the way of complete surrender. Amen.

Incidental Illustrations of the Economy of Salvation, Its Doctrines and Duties (Boston, MA: S. Chism Franklin Printing House, 1833).

Day 4

A Religion of the Heart

READ ROMANS 10:9–11; 1 PETER 3:4

It is my highest happiness to see the reign of Jesus Christ extending itself in the hearts of God's people. An external religion has too much usurped the place of religion of the heart. The ancient saints—Abraham, Isaac, Jacob, Enoch, Job—lived interiorly with God. The reign of Christ on earth is nothing more or less than the subjection of the whole soul to Himself.

Alas! The world is opposed to this reign. Many pray, "Thy will be done on earth as it is in heaven," but they are unwilling to be crucified to the world and to their sinful lusts. God designs to bring His children—naturally rebellious—through the desert of crucifixions, through the temptations in the wilderness, into the promised land. But how many rebel and choose rather to be bondslaves in Egypt rather than suffer the reductions of their sensual appetites.

—*Madame Jeanne Marie Guyon*
1989

> *Lord, help me to comprehend the hidden kingdom of the heart where You rule and reign. Enlighten me to see that it is this secret kingdom in which You establish Your throne, and from which You direct my path. In Your precious name. Amen.*

Pentecost in My Soul, (Springfield, MO: Gospel Publishing House, 1989).

Day 5
Enter In

READ MATTHEW 6:6; 13:18–23; ROMANS 10:10

Since Jesus Christ appeared on earth, there is a general belief that the kingdoms of this world will ultimately be subject to His dominion. But we may ask, "Who hastens His coming by now yielding up his or her own heart to His entire control?"

Our Lord imposed no rigorous ceremonies on His disciples. He taught them to enter into the closet, to retire within the heart, to speak but few words, to open their hearts to receive the descent of the Holy Spirit.

The holy Sabbath has not only an external, but a deeply spiritual, meaning. It symbolizes the rest of the holy soul, in union with God. Oh, that all Christians might know the coming of Jesus Christ in the soul . . . might live in God and God in them!

—*Madame Jeanne Marie Guyon*
1989

Lord, I wish to enter into that secret place of the heart—that closet—where the Holy Spirit resides day in, day out, in constant union with You. I wish to live in You, and You in me, so teach me that walk, Lord. In Jesus' name. Amen.

Pentecost in My Soul, (Springfield, MO: Gospel Publishing House, 1989).

Weekend

Going Down

READ PROVERBS 22:4; MATTHEW 23:1–12

Jordan means "going down," and there will ever be a "going down" before the "going through," and the receiving of the mantle of power. But no matter how precipitous the descent, or how lowly and humble the pathway through which our Lord may lead, let us ever remember that it is the pathway of humility that leads us to the place of power. It's the "going down" that leads to the "going up"—the going down into the realization of our own need, and that emptying out of self that brings down the mantle of power, and the filling with the Spirit of Elijah—the Holy Ghost. Falter not, beloved, and if the depths affright, just . . .

Ask the Savior to help you,
Comfort, strengthen, and keep you;
He is willing to aid you,
He will carry you through.

—*Aimee Semple McPherson*
November 1923

Lord, I willingly "go down" to Jordan. I humble myself before You, realizing that any mantle of power I may one day receive must be bestowed by You, and I cannot earn it or work to achieve it. Teach me to lean on You, for it is You who will eventually take me through the promised land. Amen.

"The Descending Mantle," *This Is That.* Used by permission of the Heritage Department of the Foursquare Gospel.

Week 9—Day 1
A God-Given Call

READ JEREMIAH 1:4–9

When I was seventeen years of age the Lord spoke these words plainly to my startled ears:

> The word of the LORD came unto me, saying, Before I formed thee . . . I knew thee; and before thou camest forth . . . I sanctified thee, and I ordained thee a prophet unto the nations. Then said I, Ah! LORD God! Behold, I cannot speak: for I am a child . . . Then the LORD put forth his hand, and touched my mouth. And the LORD said unto me, Behold, I have put my words in thy mouth (Jer. 1:4–9).

At first it seemed too astounding to be true that the Lord would ever call such a simple, unworthy girl as I to preach the gospel. But the call and ordination were so real, that although later set apart and ordained by the saints of God, the memory of my little bedroom, flooded with the glory of God as He spoke those words, has always been to me my real ordination.

—*Aimee Semple McPherson*
1966

Thank You, Father, for the call on my life. I praise You that as I seek Your direction, You guide me to fulfill that glorious plan. Amen.

The Personal Testimony of Aimee Semple McPherson (Los Angeles, CA: Heritage Committee, 1966, Revised 1997). Used by permission of the Heritage Department of the Foursquare Gospel.

Day 2

A Missionary's Widow

READ MARK 12:41–44; 2 TIMOTHY 2:7–8

There I was, in widow's weeds at nineteen and with a baby. Finding that I was a missionary's widow, the ship's passengers [from China] began to plead, "Please conduct services for us! Sunday at least." So each Lord's day while we were on the Pacific, the saloon was filled with people.

I didn't attempt to preach, just played the piano, led the passengers in song, read the Bible—read a bit and cried a bit—but when I gathered the children for Sunday school, their parents hovered around and tears glistened in the eyes of many. Whether it was the knowledge of my recent loss, or just what, I know not, but the captain said he had never seen a minister receive such attention.

Upon disembarking in San Francisco, someone touched my arm. Turning, I saw the purser. He pushed an envelope into my hand. "Here's something the passengers asked me to give you." That envelope contained sixty-seven dollars, the solution to my problem of how I would reach New York and relatives.

—*Aimee Semple McPherson*
1966

Father, thank You for the sacrificial giving of Spirit-filled women who have gone before; they gave everything they had. May I learn from their lives, and give myself to You with that same abandon. Amen.

The Personal Testimony of Aimee Semple McPherson (Los Angeles, CA: Heritage Committee, 1966, Revised 1997). Used by permission of the Heritage Department of the Foursquare Gospel.

Day 3
Not Too Many Miracles

READ EXODUS 20:14–16

Miracles happened wherever Jesus went. But miracles do not happen in the churches of today—not often, not many, not unless a church is tremendously transfused with the Spirit of God. Most churches are dying of dry-rot in the same way that Ananias and Sapphira died, only more slowly, more gradually. When church members break the eighth and ninth commandments as Ananias and Sapphira did, something in them dies, some spiritual vitality fades away. There is within their hearts the uneasiness of a secret guilt, and they are so uncomfortable about it that they either try to reason it away or try to forget it.

Then it only goes deeper into the unconscious, and a door is closed between them and God.

—*Agnes Sanford*
1969

Lord, forgive me for transgressions that may even include breaking Your commandments. Cleanse me of all sin and restore me to right-standing with You. Then, once my heart is cleansed, flow Your miracle-working power through me for Your glory. Amen.

The Healing Power of the Bible (New York: J. B . Libbincott Company, 1969).

Day 4
A Slow Death

READ MATTHEW 5:22; COLOSSIANS 3:1–10

When a person nourishes within hate and anger and refuses to forgive or be forgiven, he is taking the first step, as Jesus said, toward the final and terrible act of murder, just as when a man indulges in brooding upon lust he is taking the first step toward adultery. Jesus warned against even taking the first step, in His great horror that people might cut themselves off from God by going all the way into active, outbreaking sin.

If all this is so, you may be thinking, *Who can stand before God?*

Why, anyone can! That is the reason Jesus came and gave His life for us! Anyone who wants to stand before God and be filled with His Spirit can say, "Lord, I'm sorry! Please forgive me and help me not to sin anymore," and can be reinstated in power and in love. The life of the Spirit will again flow through. But if the person will not say this—if the person holds out against God—then a slow death begins.

—*Agnes Sanford*
1969

> *Lord, help me to both forgive and to be forgiven.*
> *Cleanse me of all unforgiveness, and reinstate me in*
> *power and in love so that the Holy Spirit will again*
> *flow through me. Thank You for such reconciliation!*
> *Amen.*

The Healing Power of the Bible (New York: J. B . Libbincott Company, 1969).

Day 5

A Miraculous Key

READ JEREMIAH 33:10–11; HEBREWS 13:13–16

I have begun to see why praise is such a miraculous key. As we begin our praising in each circumstance, ever-fresh insights follow. This much I already see. . . . Just as a genius in mathematics can skip over many interim plodding steps to get the answer to the algebra or calculus problem, even so praise is the genius-shortcut route to our answer—God. This is because praise is faith in action, faith in its most vigorous form. When we praise . . .

. . . We are letting self go by turning our backs (through an act of will) on the problem of grief where self has been most involved.

. . . We stop fighting the evil or less-than-good circumstances.

With that, resentment goes . . . self-pity goes.

Perspective comes.

We have turned our backs on the problem and are looking steadily at God.

—*Catherine Marshall LeSourd*
1974

Lord, I choose to praise You, and with that praise I receive the miraculous key to greater insight and understanding of the deep things of God. In Jesus' name. Amen.

Something More (New York: Avon Books, 1974).

Weekend

Contemplating Candy

READ GALATIANS 5:22–25; TITUS 2:11–14

Last night at bedtime I ate several pieces of candy, which was wrong from every point of view: pure gratification of self's momentary desire.

This morning I could not worship the Lord. Something was coming between us. Then the Spirit spoke gently, "Deny yourself . . . pick up your cross daily and follow Me." It was as if He were putting His finger on the words, "Deny yourself." I had even noticed them particularly in that passage. I wasn't even certain those two words were there. So I looked up the verse; they were there all right. I also got illumination on the rest of the passage: "For whoever wants to save his [higher, spiritual, eternal] life, will lose it [the lower, natural, temporal life which is lived only on earth]" Mark 8:35, AMP).

I saw that Jesus is here simply stating a fact of life. If I want to lose weight, I must give up the lower desire for stuffing my mouth in order to attain the higher desire of a fit, healthy body. If I want to write a book, I must give up the use of my time for other things. For the first time I glimpse the rationale of certain spiritual exercises, such as fasting. *Lord, teach me!*

—*Catherine Marshall LeSourd*
1974

Amen!

A Closer Walk (New York: Avon Books, 1987).

Week 10—Day 1

Storms

READ MATTHEW 14:25–33

Storms are always raging, because there are the two forces continually fighting—Jesus, the Master, and the storms of the devil. Consider the storm raging when Peter stepped out of the boat to meet Jesus on the water.

The storm was no greater when Peter observed Jesus walking on the water than most other storms. The storm was no bigger than ever; the devil just made it appear larger. The power of God didn't fail. Faith failed! Some folks like to talk of Peter's sinking. I want to talk about Peter walking.

It pays great dividends to keep one's eyes on Jesus. The powers of hell are always raging and tearing against the command of our Lord. In moments of faith we can walk calmly through the storms. There is something unseen that holds up our feet, when there is nothing seen on which to stand or walk. So let's talk about Peter walking—walking on water!

—*Mildred Wicks*
n.d.

Thank You, Jesus, for peace in the midst of life's storms. Thank You for the gift of faith that even at times enables me to follow Your example—and walk upon the water! It is You who upholds me and keeps me from sinking! Thank You! Amen!

The Dawn of a Better Day (Tulsa, OK: Standard Publishing).

Day 2

"My Pentecostal Baptism"

READ ACTS 1:1–5; 4:31–33

How thankful I am for the wonderful baptism of the Holy Ghost and for what it has meant to me all through my Christian life. And I have always been grateful to God that when I received my baptism I did not know too much about the teaching concerning it—as to how it could be received or what it would do for one who did not receive.

Not that a perfect understanding of the Pentecostal blessing would not be helpful to the one who was seeking, but for me, I was glad it was an experience of just hungering and thirsting to know more of Him.

He drew me and I followed on,
Charmed to confess His Voice divine.

—Helen Innes Wannenmacher
March 1962

Father, thank You for the Holy Spirit's baptism. I praise You for the Holy Spirit, present within me—my Teacher, Friend, Comforter, and the One who guides me closer to You. Amen.

Pentecost in My Soul (Springfield, MO: Gospel Publishing House, 1989).

Day 3
In Darkness

READ PSALM 18:11; 112:4; 139:7–12

Oh, the precious lessons of faith and patience of ten or twelve years shut in with God! How Joseph's "taste" was changed and his "scent" became as sweet spices—"myrrh, aloes, and cassia," like unto our blessed Lord of whom Joseph was a type.

He spent those years in prison, in darkness, and the darkness produced its work. When the photographer wishes to develop his pictures, he puts them in the dark, and I have heard that the best way to teach the little canaries to sing is to cover their cage, shutting out all light. So our Father often develops His image in us in the darkness.

—Miss Alice B. Garrigus
March 1926

Lord, cause Your image to be developed in me, and help me to see that even during great periods of what I perceive as restriction and spiritual darkness, You are at work forming Christ in me! In Jesus' name. Amen.

Day 4

A Simple Wish

READ JAMES 5:14–16

Uncertain prayer is no prayer at all but a simple wish. No one has a right to pray absolutely for a thing, without knowing first whether it is according to the will of God. Because He "bare our sins in His own body on the tree," we know it is not His will that we should bear them; because He "Himself took our infirmities and bore our sicknesses," and moreover "healed all that were sick," that these words might be fulfilled, we know that His will is to take them away!

The "prayer of faith" excludes the "if." So long as an "if" remains, there remains a doubt in the heart, and he who prays has not the faith of God.

—Mrs. M. Baxter
n.d.

> Lord, help me to know Your will for Your children, and thus eliminate the "ifs" from my praying. I want answers, not simple wishing, and I want most of all to fulfill Your plan for my life. In Jesus' name. Amen.

Triumphs of Faith.

Day 5
The "Ram Part"

READ GENESIS 22

A friend from Dallas has had quite a bit of experience with spiritual warfare, and one of the helpful facts he gave me is that when we're engaged in these battles energy is sapped from us and we are very prone to depression. Exactly my state for the last two months!

He also painted a very vivid picture of Genesis 22. As Abraham and Isaac were toiling up Mount Moriah, Satan must have been tempting Abraham every few minutes: *Surely you did not hear God correctly! Sacrifice your son and heir? Why should you do such an evil thing? Why, Isaac was God's special gift to you in your wife's old age. You're probably just getting senile!*

But at that very moment that Abraham was struggling with his thoughts, the ram was traveling up the other side of the Mount, and God was preparing the way of escape.

My friend's message was, God is always working on the "ram part"—the escape, God's own way out.

— *Catherine Marshall LeSourd*
1974

> *Lord, I choose to obey You, knowing that even when You seem to require a hard thing, You are Yourself preparing the way out that will be a great blessing to me. Keep me from temptation that I may press through to receive the blessing! In Jesus' name. Amen.*

A Closer Walk (New York: Avon Books, 1986).

Weekend

How Fear May Be Healed

READ 2 TIMOTHY 1:7; 1 JOHN 4:18

One of the ways of defeating this fear is to discover the unfailing, constant love and acceptance of Jesus Christ. When we learn that Jesus knows everything we have said, felt, or done, and loves us unconditionally, the cold grip of rejection is broken. It often takes an experience of unconditional love from another person to open the way to the experience of Christ's love. Jesus is the foundation of all answers to every problem. He is the Conqueror of every fear in life. To the degree that we can believe with our minds and hearts that we are loved by Jesus we will be free of fear.

—*Ruth Carter Stapleton*
1977

> *Lord, help me to receive Your unconditional love, then to express it to others as You conquer fear in and through me. In Jesus' name. Amen.*

The Experience of Inner Healing (Waco, TX: Work Books, 1977).

Week 11—Day 1

Try the Spirits

READ 1 JOHN 4:1–6

There are many kinds of power, and many spirits going out in the world today; and we are told to try the spirits; they are many. Everything is revealed by God through the blessed Holy Ghost. There is only one Spirit we want anything to do with—not our own spirit, nor any other spirit, but the Spirit of the living God.

As many as are led by the Spirit, they are the sons of God, and He will lead us into all truth. He will lead us to where we can get the truth. The child of God will be led into the baptism of the Holy Ghost and fire, which is the Pentecostal baptism.

Then we can go from one deep thing to another. The Holy Ghost is sent to us by Jesus Christ, and all spiritual gifts come through the Holy Ghost. Jesus said He shall not speak of Himself, but of His Father; He will speak to you and show you the things to come.

We believe it. Glory to God!

—*Maria Woodworth-Etter*
September 1921

Thank You, Lord, for the baptism of the Holy Ghost and fire. I praise You that by the Holy Spirit, I shall be empowered to try the spirits and to receive only that which pertains to You! Thank You for the gift of discernment! Amen!

"Spirit-Filled Sermons," *Triumphs of Faith.*

Day 2
The Voice of God

READ PSALM 29:4–9; JOHN 10:2–5

Unless you hear the voice of God, the voice of the natural man will make you attribute what you see to excitement, or to some other power. When the Holy Ghost is poured out there are always two classes—one is convinced and convicted, and accepts it; the other says, "If I accept, I will have to lead a different life, and be a gazing stock for the world, and suffer persecution." They are not willing to pay the price, so they begin to draw back.

—*Maria Woodworth-Etter*
September 1921

> *Father, help me to hear Your voice so that when I see You operate in the power of the Holy Spirit I will not begin to doubt and then to despise Your work on earth. Help me to clearly hear You so that I will receive Your works with joy. In Jesus' name. Amen.*

"Spirit-Filled Sermons," *Triumphs of Faith*.

Day 3
These Last Eventful Days

READ 2 PETER 3:1–13

Every thoughtful person in these last eventful days realizes that the prophecies that speak of the winding up of this age are being fulfilled to the letter. The sick are being healed in Jesus' name. The love of many is growing cold. The latter rain, foretold by Joel, is falling in every land. Hallelujah! These are just a few of the many signs that this age is coming to a close, and that Jesus is coming soon.

O awake, Christians, awake! Let the eyes of the blind be opened; let the deaf ears be unstopped, for Jesus is coming. . . . An open door hath been set before thee, but it is slowly, surely closing.

O awake, thou that slumberest! Make haste and press through the door, for He that shall come, *will* come, and will not tarry! Time is passing—the last hours, with their golden opportunities, are slipping by. Soon, and very soon, He will appear. Be definite. Be zealous. Be instant in season and out.

—*Mrs. J. F. Ormsby*
April 1925

Lord, help me to take advantage of these golden End-Time opportunities—opportunities to set my personal house in order, then to preach the gospel to others so that when I stand before You, I will have sheaves to lay at Your feet. In Jesus' name. Amen.

Life and Testimony: Biography of Mrs. M. B. Woodworth-Etter (Indianapolis, IN: August Feick, 1925).

Day 4
Time Is Short

READ 1 THESSALONIANS 5:1–11

Time is so short. Each setting sun brings us one day nearer the catching up of the triumphant body who shall rise to meet the Lord in the air. It will be a body of over-comers, who have washed their robes in the blood of the Lamb; who have been tested, shaken, and proved, who will have come up through tribulations, who are now in the bridal party going to the Marriage Supper of the Lamb. Hallelujah!

Will you not yield yourself as never before, and instead of complaining of the testings in your life, cry unto Him?

> Strip me, Lord, of everything
> Of this world, and self, and sin,
> That I may see the coming king
> And a crown of glory win.

> —*Mrs. J. F. Ormsby*
> *April 1925*

So be it, Lord. Give me the grace necessary to remain steady in the trials and testings. I desire to stand before You with crowns to present at Your feet. Amen.

Life and Testimony: Biography of Mrs. M. B. Woodworth-Etter (Indianapolis, IN: August Feick, 1925).

Day 5

The Perils of Preaching

READ 2 CORINTHIANS 11:23–30

During the two winters that I preached in Florida, the tent was pitched not only in Jacksonville and Tampa but in St. Petersburg, Orlando, Palm Beach, Miami, and as far south as Key West.

Interesting incidents come trooping back to mind—the nights of battling winds and water-soaked canvas, the swinging of the little sledgehammers with blistered hands, hair streaming wet in the driving rain, the experience with hundreds of school children who crawled in under our tent in Key West when it was pitched on the schoolgrounds, nights of journeying into the swamps of Georgia when armies of mosquitoes nearly ate us alive. . . . There was the experience, while crossing the continent, when our car was stuck in a windswept field of mud at two-thirty in the morning. Chilled to the bone, we resorted to the solution which only a woman could think of: We removed our petticoats and sweaters and, tying them around the wheels, flapped our way a few miles further.

—*Aimee Semple McPherson*
1927

Lord, help me to weather peril with the same grace and faith and fortitude as the Spirit-led women who have gone before me. Strengthen me, O Lord! Amen.

In the Service of the King (New York: Boni and Liveright, 1927). Used by permission of the Heritage Department of the Foursquare Gospel.

Weekend

More Perils

READ 2 TIMOTHY 3:10–17

The same night we were hopelessly stuck again and were forced to leave the children in the closely buttoned car while I slushed through the mud to the nearest railroad junction in search of help, with only a collapsible lantern with a sputtering candle inside for light.

Failing to obtain help until morning, I sat in the car all night, huddling a baby on each arm while the wind howled dismally over the unbroken reaches of the prairie.

Then there was the time when far out in the country the radiator froze and the steamroller came along and supplied us with hot water to thaw it out.

There were times when the little sloping automobile tent that covered the folding bed that was clamped to the running board froze stiff from our breath upon it.

It were far better, I think, to pass over the more tragic moments with lightest strokes and dwell upon those glorious altar calls where sinners found the Christ and upon the services of prayer where the sick were healed.

—*Aimee Semple McPherson*
1927

Lord, help me to remember always that, no matter the personal cost, it is soulwinning, and my love for others, that must motivate me. Keep me focused on what matters, and help me to pass over the tragic moments with lightest strokes. Amen.

In the Service of the King (New York: Boni and Liveright, 1927). Used by permission of the Heritage Department of the Foursquare Gospel.

Week 12—Day 1
Shimmering, Silver Nets

READ 1 CORINTHIANS 13

We may stand for the fundamentals of the gospel, for the inspiration of Scripture, the virgin birth of Jesus Christ, the Atonement, the Resurrection, and our Lord's return; we may preach it right from the shoulder. If we just make our preaching theology, even though our theory is absolutely correct, and have not the love, some way we do not get results.

Sometimes when preaching I have not the love I ought to have. I am not setting myself up as an example; Jesus is the example. Yet with that little love He has given me, sometimes when I am preaching to sinners, my heart is bleeding for them. I am trying to blink back the tears, trying to keep on smiling, yet my heart is breaking with longing to see them come to Jesus while I talk of His goodness, glory, mercy, and love. I feel as though a beautiful, shimmering, silver net is going out, out, out. Then at a certain time in my sermon, I see the shimmering, silver love net dropping around the people. Then at the altar call I fairly feel the tugging of nets full to the bursting as strong and willing hands help me pull these souls to land.

—*Aimee Semple McPherson*
November 1923

Lord, please fill me with Your love. May it go out from me as a shimmering, silver net, capturing souls for Your kingdom. In Jesus' name. Amen.

This Is That. Used by permission of the Heritage Department of the Foursquare Gospel.

Day 2
Wind and Tongues of Flame

READ JOHN 14:26; 16:7; ACTS 2:1–4

With rushing wind and tongues of flame, descended the Holy Ghost upon the hundred and twenty on the Day of Pentecost and filled them with His Spirit. They had seen the ascending Christ, had received the descending Holy Spirit. The mantle of power that had descended from God out of heaven and fallen upon Jesus in the Jordan had now descended upon, and did abide upon, the believers who were to carry on His work.

Even as it was necessary for Elijah to be caught up before his mantle could fall on Elisha, so it was necessary with our Lord and Master, who said, "It is expedient for you that I go away: for if I go not away, the Comforter will not come unto you; but if I depart, I will send Him unto you."

The perseverance, going-through, and expectancy of Elisha were rewarded. The obedience, prayer, and waiting of the disciples in the upper room were also rewarded, as will be the earnest following after the fullness of the Spirit.

—*Aimee Semple McPherson*
November 1923

Lord, I press through in prayer, perseverance, and obedience to receive the mantle of power—the Holy Spirit. Fill me fresh each day, Lord, with the Holy Spirit. In Jesus' name. Amen.

This Is That. Used by permission of the Heritage Department of the Foursquare Gospel.

Day 3

Unity in Holiness

READ EPHESIANS 4:1–3; HEBREWS 12:14

The apostle speaks of "the unity of the spirit." Holiness gives that unity. When we enter within the veil through the blood of the everlasting covenant, we meet on the ground where—

> Names, and sects, and parties fall,
> And Christ alone is all in all.

Yes, you are my sister in Christ! We have been begotten together in the bowels of Jesus. One says, "Spiritual relationships are often stronger than those of nature." And why should they not be? For natural ties, apart from religious influences, have their origin and end in the present state; whereas spiritual relationships have their origin in the Eternal God, the Infinite Source of life and happiness, and must, if rightly cherished, endure as long as God Himself endures.

—*Phoebe Palmer*
1835

> *Lord, help me to form spiritual relationships with my sisters in Christ, and to enjoy the unity of the Spirit that only the Holy Spirit can provide. Use me, Lord, as an instrument of unity within the body of Christ. In Jesus' name. Amen.*

Incidental Illustrations of the Economy of Salvation, Its Doctrines and Duties (Boston, MA: S. Chism Franklin Printing House, 1833).

Day 4
"The Just Shall Live By Faith"

READ HABBAKUK 2:4; ROMANS 1:17–19

If your faith was to depend on your variable feelings, instead of on the Word of God, the hope of being without variableness would be small. But can you not make up your mind to believe God irrespective of your feelings?

In the name of the Lord, I ask whether you will not now resolve to live a life of faith; for it is written, "The just shall live by faith."

—*Phoebe Palmer*
1835

Lord, increase my faith so that I will not stagger through unbelief. I desire to live by faith and to walk by faith. Amen.

Incidental Illustrations of the Economy of Salvation, Its Doctrines and Duties (Boston, MA: S. Chism Franklin Printing House, 1833).

Day 5

The Confession of the Mouth

READ ROMANS 10:9–13

The Author and Finisher of your faith is now waiting to hear the confession of your mouth. Angels in heaven, saints on earth, and the spirits of the just made perfect, now disembodied, love to hear God praised for His wonderful works. Shall they now hear an acknowledgment of your faith? If in your heart you believe, now say:

Faith in thy name thou seest I have,
For thou that faith hast wrought;
Dead souls thou callest from the grave,
And speakest worlds from nought,
The thing surpasses all my thought,
Yet faithful is my Lord;
Through unbelief I stagger not,
For God hath spoke the word.
'Tis done, thou dost this moment save,
With full salvation bless;
Redemption through the blood I have,
And spotless love and peace.

—*Phoebe Palmer*
1835

Lord, I believe—and because I believe, I confess You with my mouth. Jesus is Lord! Thank You, Jesus, for saving my soul. Thank You for the gift of the Holy Spirit! Amen.

Incidental Illustrations of the Economy of Salvation, Its Doctrines and Duties (Boston, MA: S. Chism Franklin Printing House, 1833).

Weekend

Precious in His Sight

READ PROVERBS 11:30; JOHN 4:34–36

Oh, the fields are white, for the harvest is great and ripe, and it is ready for the gospel sickle; oh, where are the laborers to gather the golden grain into the Master's garner?

The world is dying, the grave is filling, hell is boasting; it will all be over soon.

God left the glorious work of saving souls in the hands of the church. What is the church? Men, women, and children. God's church is a workshop; no idlers allowed there. There should be bills posted: "To work, to work, everyone at a post." The work is great and the time is short. We are putting up a building for God; everyone has a part in this building. If we cannot be a pillar or a cornerstone, let us be a spike or a nail or a brick. Let us not despise the day of small things. Whatever we do for Jesus, with the right motive, is precious in His sight.

—*Maria Woodworth-Etter*
1916

Lord, I want to help You build Your church. I want to be a brick or a nail if I can't be a pillar or a cornerstone. Reveal my post, so that I may faithfully occupy it, and use me to win souls. In Jesus' name. Amen.

"Women's Right in the Gospel," *Signs and Wonders* (Bartlesville, OK: Oak Tree Publications, 1916).

Week 13—Day 1
Resist the Devil

READ JAMES 4:1–6; 1 PETER 5:8–11

"Resist the devil and he will flee from you." On every hand we find those who have come up to the point where they met opposition of the enemy, and instead of resisting the devil, they have retreated before him and have lost the victory.

Undoubtedly those who read these words will have learned to resist the devil in his endeavors to make them commit sin in its grosser forms. But when we realize that whatsoever is not of faith is sin, we shall see how at every point we need to resist the devil. It is because our blessed Lord on Calvary has conquered Satan that we have the continual power in Jesus' name to resist the devil. When thoughts of unbelief arise they are Satan's own suggestions, and we must not listen. Likewise, when thoughts of discouragement arise, we must not entertain them for an instant. We must say in faith, "The Lord rebuke thee, Satan!" Or boldly say, "I resist you, Satan, in the name of Jesus who is your conqueror!"

—Carrie Judd Montgomery
September 1944

Lord, teach me to resist the devil in the small things as well as the great ones; help me to reject his encroachment into my thoughts and lifestyle, and quicken to me when it's time to resist the enemy in the power and name of Jesus Christ. Amen.

"Don't Answer," *Triumphs of Faith.*

Day 2
Don't Listen

READ EPHESIANS 6:11–13; REVELATION 12:10–11

The enemy gets a stronghold in the minds of people often because they listen to his suggestions instead of refusing them. As soon as we are conscious that it is the enemy speaking, we must not allow him to finish his sentence.

When I said this to a Christian sister, she replied, "I thought I ought to let him finish his sentence so I would know how to answer him." We are not to answer him at all; we are to refuse to let him talk to us, and then turn him over to Christ, who is God's answer to him to all eternity.

If we try to answer Satan, we shall get into as much trouble as Eve did when she listened to him and tried to answer him. Satan is very wise and is too much for our wisdom, but not too much for the Lord.

—*Carrie Judd Montgomery*
September 1944

> *Lord, I choose not to listen to the enemy next time he comes to me. Help me to turn him quickly over to You, rather than trying to answer him myself. I praise You, Lord, for eternal victory over the enemy. In Jesus' name. Amen.*

"Don't Answer," *Triumphs of Faith.*

Day 3
Give Up

READ 1 CORINTHIANS 2:16; HEBREWS 12:3

Dear troubled one, "wearied and faint in your mind," give up today your own mind and your own thoughts and reckon by faith that you have the mind of Christ. Thus shall you know His wonderful rest. We have often met dear ones upon whom the enemy was trying to put a spirit of fear, through press of trouble and care.

The verse found in 2 Timothy 1:7 will quiet such fears, and we read, "God hath not given us the spirit of fear; but of power, and of love, and of a sound mind." It is the enemy and not our loving Father who gives "the spirit of fear," and we must resist it through the blood of Jesus and through His all-prevailing name.

—*Carrie Judd Montgomery*
October 1945

Lord, help me to resist the spirit of fear with the blood of Jesus and the power of His name. Amen.

"The Mind of Christ," *Triumphs of Faith.*

Day 4
The Secret Place

READ PSALM 91

There is a secret place within the holy of holies under the very cover of Christ's wing—a place where we always have access to the mercy seat. It's a place of unbroken communion; a place where our spirits are made so spotless by the blood of Jesus that He can always smile upon us. This is the "secret place of the Most High." This is the life hid with Christ in God.

Some of you have at last come to a difficulty that you felt even God could not meet, and in your unbelief you did not know Him as the One who had all might. That was because you were not abiding in the secret place of the Most High.

Oh, Beloved! Let us not be satisfied with anything short of this: There is a holy place, but there is also a holy of holies. If you are not satisfied with anything less, God will give you His uttermost salvation.

—*Carrie Judd Montgomery*
October 1940

> *Lord, lead me to Your secret place where I can be hid beneath Your wings and where I will experience unbroken communion with You. In Jesus' name. Amen.*

Triumphs of Faith.

Day 5

Learning to Lean

READ PSALM 6; MATTHEW 11:28–30

The more He permits us to feel our helplessness, the more we learn to lean on Him.

"I will say of the Lord, He is my refuge and my fortress: my God; in Him will I trust." Here we see that we are to confess our faith before the feeling comes. I will say it on His Word, I will say it to my own heart, I will say it to the devil, and he will have to flee. Here is where our consecrated willpower comes in. "In Him I *will* trust." A surrendered will is a will given over to God, so that He can work in it, to will of His good pleasure. I *will* trust in Him, no matter what comes, no matter what I have to go through. I will put my will over on His side, and let Him work out His will in and through me.

—Carrie Judd Montgomery
June 1932

Lord, teach me to lean on You. I choose to put my will over to You today to use as You see fit. I will trust You, no matter what. In Jesus' name. Amen.

"Feathers," *Triumphs of Faith.*

Weekend

All Things Work for Good

READ JOB 7:17–18; ROMANS 8:28–29; 1 PETER 3:11–16

God tries us, proves us, and establishes us. It is not by a quick process. "He shall sit, as a Refiner and Purifier of silver." He sits down to His work. He will wait years with you over a single lesson, or He will get you through it at once if you are willing to take the quicker process and hotter fire.

How touching is the love that will take so much trouble with these little matters. No wonder Job says, "What is man, that thou shouldst magnify him? And that thou shouldest set thine heart upon him? And that Thou shouldst visit him every morning, and try him every moment!"

Yes, every moment the great Refiner is waiting to add some new touch to your strength and beauty and fit you for a higher place in His eternal life. We are so prone to think that these that come to us are accidents, incidents, mishaps, or personal injuries from personal hands; but after awhile we learn that His hand is above every other hand, and His love above every hateful blow.

—*Carrie Judd Montgomery*
June 1932

Lord, help me to see Your hand in every trial, and to understand that it is You who truly causes all things— great and small, joyful and painful, helpful and hurtful—to work together for good, because You love me. In Jesus' name. Amen.

"Feathers," *Triumphs of Faith.*

Part 2—
Spring

. . . . A time
to plant . . .

—*Ecclesiastes 3:2,* NKJV

Week 14—Day 1
Renewed Youth

READ ISAIAH 40

As the eagle grows old its upper beak grows very long and curls under, so much so as to lock into the under one, thus preventing the poor bird from taking its food. It gets weaker, and death seems imminent. But there is something that the bird itself must do—find a rough rock upon which it must rub off the upper beak. This process is painful, and the bird will not do it if it can avoid it. The other eagles, perceiving its plight and knowing the remedy, encourage their comrade by bringing the choicest morsels of food they can find, and placing them in front of the poor, old, starving eagle.

At last the look and smell of the food drive the bird to desperation as it makes a determined effort to rid itself of the hindrance that prevents its eating. In the process of rubbing, the beak falls off and, behold!—there is a new beak underneath. The bird immediately begins to eat, its youth is renewed, strong life returns, and the dying eagle enters a new lease on life. The Lord says it shall be thus with those who believe His Word.

—*Mrs. M. Martin*
n.d.

Lord, remove every hindrance that keeps me from eating the food—Your Word—that will restore me. Nourish me and give me a new lease on life in the Spirit. Amen.

"Renewed Youth," *Triumphs of Faith.*

Day 2
You Are Valuable!

READ JOHN 3:16; ROMANS 5:6–11

A drunkard, lying in a gutter clutching his bottle, was attracted to a Christian who was sharing the gospel on the street. The preacher emphasized the importance of life and was trying to help people realize their value.

The drunkard was touched by the idea that God valued him that much. It had never occurred to him that his life had value to God. When the street preacher concluded, the drunk man called out: "Sir, I want to be saved. But I am a drunk. I am no good."

The preacher said, "Friend, God loves you like you are. He created you like Himself. He has already paid to redeem you. . . . Just accept Him and His love for you!"

"I do, I do," the drunk man said. And he was transformed.

The miracle began when he realized that he was valuable to God. When you, as a woman, accept your own self-value, you can begin to discover real life for women. Then you can accept God's value of others and you can begin to share that life with them.

—*Daisy Washburn Osborn*
1991

> *Lord, help me to realize my own self-value as I comprehend the price You paid to redeem me from my sins. Teach me to value others and to share the life of the Spirit with those around me. Amen.*

New Life for Women, (Tulsa, OK: OSFO Publishers, 1991), 71–74.

Day 3

"Not My Will, but Thine . . ."

READ COLOSSIANS 3:3–4

In a vision, I entered Gethsemane, and was about to drink a cup that was very distasteful to me. I found myself saying, "O Lord, let this cup pass from me."

An agony of intense suffering came over me, but my spirit was quieted when I was told by an inner voice, "Child, you are fellowshiping the sufferings of Christ. You are not alone. I am taking you through." Then I began to repeat, "Not my will, but Thine be done."

This went on for some time, and I sensed I was about to be taken through the crucifixion. I felt the pain of nails piercing my hands and feet. Again, I was shrinking from disgrace and humiliation connected with the cross, but the tender voice of Jesus quieted every nerve, and a sweet peace took possession of me. He assured me that I was being made conformable to His death, and that He would never leave me nor forsake me. What a yieldedness entered my being! I began to feel that it was an honor, rather than a disgrace, to share His sufferings on the cross.

—*Sister Christine*
1906

Lord, help me to understand that the way of the cross is the crucified life, and that to be crucified means to die—die to self—but live to You! And that is no disgrace but an honor! Amen!

From Mary Campbell Willson, *The Obedience of Faith*, (Victory House, Inc., 1993).

Day 4
The "Death Route"

READ COLOSSIANS 3:4

Yes, I saw myself hanging there; I heard the slanderous talk of those watching me die. Some were criticizing my life, while others were praising my virtues, telling of all the service I had accomplished for my Lord, and although I knew I was hanging on the cross, I was looking at the dead figure hanging there, from whom no response was coming.

I found myself saying, "She is dead, she is dead." Then I realized that I was going to be buried. I was lowered into an open grave and a horror of darkness swept over me. This lasted for a while, after which that scene changed and I heard voices saying, "The resurrection morning has come." I expected to see myself emerge from the grave, but to my amazement, a man came forth and I saw Jesus. I cried out, "Where am I?" And the answer came, "Your life is hidden with Christ in God."

I promised my Lord that, by His grace, I would go forth, taking a "death route."

—*Sister Christine*
1906

Lord, resurrection is not possible except there first be crucifixion. What has not died cannot be risen; therefore, regardless of discomfort or disgrace, I choose the "death route." Cover me in grace and take me through to glory. In Jesus' name. Amen.

From Mary Campbell Willson, *The Obedience of Faith*, (Victory House, Inc., 1993).

Day 5

Think of It!

Read Deuteronomy 32:9; Ephesians 1:16–18

Think of it! The Bible says that God has been made rich because we who are Christ's have been given to Him! God is interested in a love relationship with us!

How wrong the church has been so often to teach new Christians that we are saved to serve God. No! We are saved primarily because He wants us for Himself. That is why He has "loved back my life from the pit of corruption and nothingness," and "cast all my sins behind [His] back" (Isa. 38:17, AMP). God isn't in the business of saving people because He needs servants to win the world for Christ, or because without us He might lose the battle against the devil. Yet, many Christians believe that they are working for a semi-impotent God who needs their help and expects them to repay Him.

The Bible never once tells us to do anything *for* God. It tells us that in His love and grace, God chose to *involve* us in what He was doing. We can work *with Him and allow Him to work* through *us. Think of it!*

—*Roxanne Brandt*
1973

> *Lord, I cease from my own efforts to "pay You back" with works for the free gift of salvation. Help me to respond in service to You from the right understanding of what it means to be involved in Your plan for mankind. In Jesus' name. Amen.*

Ministering to the Lord, (Springdale, PA: Whitaker House, 1973), 14–16.

Weekend
Our First Obligation

READ LUKE 10:38–42

God could have evangelized this world with a group of angels, but He chose to give us the pleasure and privilege of working together with Him to accomplish that end.

Unfortunately, because the church so often teaches that we are here first to serve God, we have an abundance of guilt-laden Marthas who are cumbered about with much anxious serving, and there is a dearth of worship-oriented Marys who have entered into the rich love relationship with God, out of which the burden for human need so naturally springs.

Jesus did not rebuke Martha's serving but her overconcern and anxious preoccupation with "things" more than with God. Service that is born of a love relationship is not anxious, but meaningful and joy-filled. Our first obligation in our relationship to God is love. Yet we have centered our attention on ministries, gifts, order, different types of programs and services, and so forth. We have centered our attention on everything except Him.

—*Roxanne Brandt*
1973

Lord, help me to center my attention on You, not on things—not on ministry, not on gifts, not on service— You! Realign me as it may be necessary so that I fulfill my first obligation to You, which is love. In Jesus' name. Amen.

Ministering to the Lord, (Springdale, PA: Whitaker House, 1973), 14–16.

Week 15—Day 1
Is It God's Will to Heal?

READ MATTHEW 9:35; MARK 6:56; JOHN 4:34

This is the one question that is asked more often than any other by those who need healing of the body and by those who oppose the truth of divine healing. No one disputes or denies that Jesus of Nazareth, the only begotten Son of the Father, more perfectly and more completely fulfilled the will of God in all His life and in all His work than anyone who has ever lived. If this be true, then when we find what Jesus did when He walked the shores of Galilee and the Judean Hills, we shall know what the will of God is.

Surely if it had not been God's will to heal the sick, Jesus would not have "healed all that were oppressed of the devil." He would not have "healed all that came to Him." He would not have "healed every sickness and every disease among the people." Since Jesus did do this and since He said of Himself, "I come to do the will of Him that sent Me," may we not take this as conclusive proof that it is God's will to heal the body of its physical pain and suffering?

—*Mrs. Raymond T. Richey*
n.d.

Lord, thank You that it's Your will to heal. I claim healing now, in Jesus' name. Amen.

Is It God's Will to Heal?, n.d.

Day 2

Out of the Mouths of Babes

READ PSALM 8

A mother, tired with watching over a sick baby, came downstairs for a moment's rest. She heard the voice of her little four-year-old girl in the hall by herself and, curious to know to whom she was talking, stopped a moment at the half-open door. She saw the little thing had pulled a chair in front of the telephone, and stood upon it. The earnestness of the child showed that she was in no playful mood. This was the one-sided conversation the mother heard, while tears stood thick in her eyes:

"Hello . . . Is Jesus there? . . . Tell Jesus I want to speak to Him . . . Well? . . . Is that You, Jesus? . . . Our baby is sick, and we want You to let it get well. Won't You, now? . . . Yes."

The little one put the earpiece back on its hook, clambered down from the chair, and with a radiant face went for her mother, who caught her in her arms.

The baby, whose life had been despaired of, began to mend that day, and got well.

—*Carrie Judd Montgomery*
n.d.

Lord, help me to esteem the prayers of my children, for their purity of heart represents the childlikeness that You require from each of us. Forgive me for ever thinking their prayers to be "cute" or ineffective. In Jesus' name. Amen.

Word and Work, n.d.

Day 3

Yield Yourself

READ JOB 16:12; PSALM 30:5

Dear suffering one, God will heal you if the conditions are right. Ask God to turn on the searchlight to see where self is keeping you away from doing His perfect will. You can have no doubts, no fears, no reasoning, no opinions of your own, but just believe and take God at His Word. Stand on it. Claim it now as your own light, and God will make it real as you test Him.

Sometimes when you have yielded all worldiness, habits, and desires to Him, there is something else. You will find that *something* is yourself, the "old man," perhaps in the form of sensitiveness or being easily offended, or having your own ideas about things. You must yield yourself so entirely and implicitly to Him that you will endure the cross, yea, more; touch the cross. Lie quietly to be nailed on it; have all props taken out from under you, that you may die to self, as Jesus had to the last three hours of His life. That this will be an aid to many who are in darkness, to show them the Way, is my heart's cry to Father!

—*Mrs. R. J. Moss*
n.d.

Lord, I believe Your Word. I stand on it, claim it, and yield myself to You, along with every preconceived notion I may have as to how You may desire to work Your plan out in my life. In Jesus' name. Amen.

From the tract, *From Bondage to Liberty: A Message on Divine Healing,* n.d.

Day 4

One Step Ahead of the Critics

READ MATTHEW 4:24; HEBREWS 12:12–14

A lot of people today are trying to stop the flow of the mighty river. They are saying, "Hold steady, now; here comes a banker, and perhaps we can get him. Here comes a doctor; keep still, and don't do anything that will drive him away." Don't imagine for a moment that you can get through to God that way!

I remember a meeting in which there was a little woman whom God had healed of very serious lung trouble. One lung had been gone and the other one badly scarred. She had received such a blessing that she could not keep still, and she shouted in every service. When she testified the tears would flow. But one day a great evangelist came. The whole town turned out, and the meeting was in full swing. This little woman was there, and I watched her. *If she gets happy, I don't know how this evangelist will take it,* I thought. Finally this little lady could contain it no longer. She began to shout, and then she started to dance in the Spirit. She went dancing down the aisle, shouting for joy. The ushers followed her, down one aisle and up the other, and could not catch her. The Holy Ghost is always one step ahead of the critics!

—*Emma Taylor*
November 1939

Lord, give me the kind of anointing that will take no note of the critics! In Jesus' name. Amen.

The Pentecostal Evangel.

Day 5

A Royal Daughter in God's Family

READ LUKE 11:9–13; 2 CORINTHIANS 6:17–18

When any believing woman begins to see herself in Christ, and confess that, she becomes a royal daughter in God's family, with all of the rights and privileges of any member of His divine household.

As a woman believer, embrace and confess these facts in a positive way:

- Christ lives in me.
- Christ dwells in my heart by faith—Christ in me, the hope of glory.
- Christ is my Life . . . but of Him am I in Christ Jesus.
- Christ Jesus is in me.

Women who are aware of their legal standing in God take their places as redeemed members of the New Testament church, marching forward in triumph.

—Daisy Washburn Osborn
1991

Lord, help me to see myself in Christ and Christ in me; I confess that with my heart and with my mouth. Help me to rise up into my rightful position in the body of Christ. Amen.

New Life for Women, (Tulsa, OK: OSFO Publishers), 176–177.

Weekend

Your Response to God's Ability

READ ROMANS 14

One day each of us will stand personally before the judgment seat of God. Yes, each of us will give an account of herself or himself to God. When the truth of Romans, chapter 14, stood out forcibly to me, I realized that I had discovered some declarations in the Bible, which, by normal church culture and by ecclesiastical tradition, are overlooked by women.

I had read Romans, chapter 14, many times, but that day I discovered the seeds of truth that would have a profound and eternal effect upon my life—and ultimately on the lives of women around the world. I realized that I, Daisy Marie Washburn Osborn, will be one of those persons gathered before the King. What I do, or do not do, for people and for my Lord in this life will determine my classification forever.

It is important to recognize that with God-given ability comes responsibility, which is simply this: Your response to God's ability.

—*Daisy Washburn Osborn*
1991

> *Lord, help me to keep my eyes fixed on You, and to walk in the light of the knowledge that what I do or don't do, in response to Your ability, for others and for You will determine my classification for eternity. In Jesus' name. Amen.*

New Life for Women, (Tulsa, OK: OSFO Publishers), 58–59.

Week 16—Day 1
A Ship Without a Pilot

READ LUKE 5

In Luke, chapter 5, Jesus—who was not a fisherman—told Simon exactly where to put his nets into the sea. Simon must have been surprised; perhaps he thought he knew just a little more than the Master about the art of fishing! Here is what Simon answered: "Master, we have toiled all the night, and have taken nothing; nevertheless at thy word, I will let down the net."

How many of us have fished all night and have caught nothing! We started with determination but the trail was so hard, and success has not crowned our efforts. We wonder what went wrong. We know we have done our best, and we are weary and discouraged.

I know what was wrong with those fishermen. They had fished all night and caught nothing because they had left Jesus on the shore! They did not have the Nazarene aboard their boat. That is the trouble; they tried to live a Christian life in their own strength. They tried to walk the way of life without a Guide. They tried to sail their ship without a Pilot.

—Anna D. Britton
August 1934

Lord, be my Pilot and Guide and help me to involve You in every facet of my life. Then I will get good results; then I will have what I need to win souls for You. Amen.

The Bridal Call-Crusader.

Day 2

We Are All Helpless

READ 1 CORINTHIANS 15:12–19

I believe that we are all helpless. We are all in the condition that Peter and his companions, James and John, were in once they let down the nets right where Jesus said and pulled multitudes of fish onboard. Simon Peter was so affected by what had happened that, realizing his own sinful condition, he fell down at Jesus' feet, saying, "Depart from me: for I am a sinful man, O Lord."

No matter what our vocation may be, we are helpless without Jesus. Without the Christ we are failures; but with Him and with His Word, we are truly successful.

I believe that the reason some people are not healed is that they fail to see in the Word the Living Christ. They fix their eyes upon the one who prays for them, and not on the Master's blessed face. If, by the eye of faith, we can behold Him who is invisible—if, by the ear of faith we can hear His voice which speaks only to the heart—then we shall enjoy the riches of God.

—*Anna D. Britton*
August 1934

Lord, I fix my eyes on You and not on the one who prays for me—not on myself, not on my prayer partner, not on my pastor or some nationally known minister. I fix my eyes on You, realizing that without You I am helpless. And now by faith, I receive my answer. In Jesus' name. Amen.

Day 3
A Morning Prayer

READ PSALM 143

In the morning will I direct my prayer unto Thee,
and will look up.
My voice shalt Thou hear in the morning,
For the day is all unknown,
And I am afraid, without Thine aid,
To face its hours alone.
Give me Thy Spirit to lead me,
Give me Thy Hands to guide.
Give me Thy living Presence
To be ever at my side.

—*Kate Knight*
April 1934

Lord, I seek You in the morning. Guide my way and lead me on prepared ground to my destiny. In Jesus' name. Amen.

"A Revelation of the Love of God," *The Pentecostal Evangel.*

Day 4

In the Bosom of the Father

READ JOHN 1

Alone in my room in Bombay early on the morning of January 28, 1908, I sat down to my regular reading for the day, beginning at John 1. When I reached verse 18 the Holy Spirit emphasized the words, "in the bosom of the Father," saying them over and over. I knelt with my face near the floor, eyes closed. Soon I seemed to see heaven full of glory and music and thrones and angels. In a short time all receded except the Father and His Son, standing alone. I marveled at the likeness of the Two, and then the words came, "The express image of His person."

I glanced at the hands of Jesus. He seemed to wish to hide the scars. Then He shook back the sleeves, and as He gave His hands to His Father, I saw the scars, not as I had imagined on the surface, but deep, like holes. The Father, with tears rolling down His face, kissed the scarred hands again and again . . . kissed the wounded feet. Afterward He arose, and Jesus buried His face in His Father's breast as the Spirit whispered to me, "In the bosom of the Father."

Weeping, I said to God, "Did You always love Him so?"

"Always," He said.

—*Kate Knight*
April 1934

Lord, thank You for a revelation of Your love—for Your Son, and for me. Thank You that those scars are there—for me. In Jesus' name. Amen.

"A Revelation of the Love of God," *The Pentecostal Evangel.*

Day 5
Why Do We Love God?

READ REVELATION 4

I once heard the story of a very elderly lady who went to visit President Abraham Lincoln one afternoon. As she entered the president's office, he arose, seated her, and asked, "How may I be of service to you, Madame?"

The little lady said, "Mr. President, I have not come to ask you for anything. I simply came to bring you this box of cookies, for I heard you enjoy them so much."

A silence followed in which tears overflowed the eyes of the president. Finally, he raised his head and spoke: "Madame, I thank you for your thoughtful gift. I am greatly moved by it. Since I have been the president, thousands of people have come to this office asking for favors and demanding things of me. You are the first person who has ever entered these premises asking no favor, and indeed, bringing a gift for me. I thank you from the bottom of my heart."

In the same way, God longs for us to come to Him for Himself, instead of simply for what He can give us.

—*Roxanne Brandt*
1973

> *Lord, I come to You in worship, glorifying You for who You are, not asking You for anything, thanking You for Your free gift of salvation and for the daily grace You pour out to enable me to walk in the Spirit. Amen.*

Ministering to the Lord, 12–14.

Weekend

Party of Seven

READ PSALM 27:9; HEBREWS 13:5–6

I was in Seattle, Washington, at the Northwest Bible College—my last meeting before I went overseas. The president of the college and his wife took me to the airport. To them I appeared to be this little woman, all alone, walking out to the airplane. The president's wife wrote a note when she got back home, stating how she had cried when she saw me walking out to that airplane all alone. I got a letter back to her right away. I wrote:

"Honey, I didn't go alone. I have an evangelistic party of seven—but let me tell you something lovely. I only have to buy one ticket, and all seven of us sit in the same seat. The Father says, 'Certainly I will be with you.' That's two. Jesus says, 'I'll never leave you nor forsake you.' That's three of us. The Holy Spirit says, 'I'll be right inside of you.' That is now four of us. The angel of the Lord encamps around about. That's five of us. Finally, goodness and mercy follow me all the days of my life. That makes seven. You see, I am not alone."

—*Hattie Hammond*
n.d.

Lord, thank You that I am not alone—that seven walk with me at all times. May I be blessed with that same lightness of heart and brightness of attitude that Sister Hattie Hammond possessed. Thank You for her message. In Jesus' name. Amen.

Audiocassette titled "Agelessness," from a chapel service at Christ for the Nations.

Week 17—Day 1
"Grace Is Sufficient"

READ PSALM 138

One beautiful young married woman began seeking the baptism . . . all at once there came a holy hush over the house. The power of God's brooding Spirit was felt in such a wonderful way that no one could speak aloud. And then she spoke: "Oh, something so sweet has come right in here," and she clasped her hands over her breast. Her face was like an angel's. Then she sank to the floor. Softly, she began singing in tongues, joyously at first; then it became a minor wail of deepest sorrow, sweet and low, with that wonderful glow on her face.

Just as she began this sad melody in tongues, her beautiful young husband stepped from a train. His foot caught, he fell, and the train passed over him, crushing his life.

The pastor and I went at once. O, praise God, in the midst of that awful trouble she sat with that same glory on her face that she had when she left the altar the night before. No outcry. No frantic giving way, but just that heavenly look on her face. She said, "Glory! Glory!"

I'll never forget it, sister; nothing but Pentecost could do that!

—*Mae E. Frey*
June 1921

Lord, fill me with Your glory so that at all times, Your grace is sufficient for me. In Jesus' name. Amen.

The Pentecostal Evangel.

Day 2

The One Who Has a Future

READ ISAIAH 43:18–19; JEREMIAH 29:21

When our thirty-four-year-old son died, I was left with a physical ache in my heart that I thought would never leave. It was there day and night. I prayed, "Lord, will this ache ever leave?"

And the Lord said to me, "The one who can release the past is the one who has a future." This seed idea began to grow in me, and I have come to learn the importance of letting go—of hurts, of injuries, of injustices, and even of the good times. The only thing that you can take into your future from your past is the knowledge that you have gained from your experiences. Your past is your teacher. Your present is your opportunity. Your future is your friend.

Never be afraid of your future. Secure it by planting good seed today. Your good future begins by making a decision for Jesus Christ. When He hooks up to your seed-planting ability, your future is indeed your friend.

—*Daisy Washburn Osborn*
1991

Lord, I release the past. Help me to plant good seeds for the future, and to embrace it—not fear it. Thank You that You are the Author of my future, and that it is for good. In Jesus' name. Amen.

New Life for Women (Tulsa, OK: OSFO Publishers, 1991).

Day 3

Sanctify Yourself

READ EXODUS 19:10; NUMBERS 11:18

Before giving the law to Moses on Mount Sinai, God said unto Moses, "Go unto the people and sanctify them today and tomorrow." At the same time, when the people murmured because they had no flesh to eat, and God yielded to their desire, before the seventy elders were appointed and before the Spirit of God rested upon them, again the command of God went forth: "Sanctify yourselves!"

For great and special occasions when the power and deliverance of God were to be signally manifested, it was but becoming that the people should be set apart, be free from all distractions, all ordinary occupation. There are times when God calls us thus apart, yet the press and crush of occupation comes upon us so overwhelmingly that it seems impossible to get free. God has permitted it, so that we may be placed in the position to choose whether God or business, God or Christian work, God or our reputation for work shall have the first claim. Before the Jordan can be crossed, there must be such a setting apart unto God.

—*Mrs. Mary Baxter*
n.d.

Lord, I sanctify myself before You. Show me what must fall away in order that I may be free to worship You in spirit and in truth. Amen.

God's People (London: Christian Herald).

Day 4
He Left Us Down Here

READ JOHN 14

There was only one person in the whole universe who received the baptism of the Holy Spirit with the manifestation of a dove. The rest of us got the fire. That fire was to purge us and cleanse us. It was to go through us and deal with us to get out of us all that sin.

A woman once said to me, "Why did God make me like this? Why did He give me a disposition like this?"

I said, "Honey, God didn't make any of us the miserable creatures that we are. Sin did that to us. What you are when you came to Jesus is the result of sin. Sin did that awful thing to us. It has made us deformed, crippled, diseased, marred, and scared in nature and disposition. It has caused mental darkness."

That's why God leaves us down here—because He wants to disentangle us out of this thing that we are caught up in. He wants to deal with us, release us, redeem us, salvage us. He wants to bring us out and make us that beautiful likeness of God. He wants to restore us; that's why He leaves us down here!

—Hattie Hammond
n.d.

Lord, thank You for leaving me down here long enough to redeem and restore me. Thank You that Your plan is to release the beauty of Christ-likeness in me. Amen.

Audiocassette titled "Give Me Your Heart," from a chapel service at Christ for the Nations.

Day 5
Dried Up

READ ISAIAH 64:6–8; JOHN 4:13–14

My mother was a beautiful Christian, but when God put a hunger and thirst in her heart for the baptism in the Holy Spirit, He dried up all her past experiences. She knew the Bible cover to cover, but when He wanted to baptize her, He had to show her that she must move on, for there was no rain where she was standing. One day she came to my room and said, "Daughter, I don't believe I ever was saved. My prayers and big talk and all my knowledge I believe are nothing, nothing but filthy rags; nothing but works. I don't believe I have ever had a real experience of salvation."

I said, "Mother, that is what God is doing to open up your soul for the baptism in the Holy Ghost. He is giving you the light of the hour, and He wants you to be separated from your old experiences, to leave them behind and go on, that you may receive the baptism in the Holy Ghost."

One night Father and I came home from meeting, and we heard someone singing like an angel. I said, "Father, listen!" He went around to where he could find the singer, and there sat Mother in the kitchen, hands raised, singing in a heavenly language.

—*Mrs. Robert A. Brown*
n.d.

Lord, fill me with that same thirst for Your Spirit, and help me to let go of past experiences. Amen.

Word and Work.

Weekend

Hallelujah, It Is Done!

READ REVELATION 21

Polly was attracted by the sound of trumpets and the beating of drums to an open-air meeting. The Salvation Army was an entirely new thing, and she looked at these people with great interest. When the meeting was over, they marched on, and she followed them to a dilapidated theater building. *Dare she go into a theater?* Looking this way and that, she slipped in.

The evangelist was Gipsy Tillie Smith, sister of the famous Salvation Army evangelist, Gipsy Rodney Smith. Polly yearned to know Christ and the power of His cleansing blood to wash away her sins. When the call was made for sinners to come down, Polly made her way from the gallery to the altar. When the assurance came that she was forgiven, Polly jumped to her feet, threw her gloves in the air, and shouted "Hallelujah! It is done!"

A young Smith Wigglesworth was in the audience. He watched the woman pray through, and heard her shout. Later he declared, "It seemed as if the inspiration of God was upon her from the very first."

—*Polly Wigglesworth*
1948

Lord, thank You that Your blood has washed away my sins. Thank You that even when I am not aware of it, You are arranging circumstances behind the scenes that will shape my future. Amen.

Stanley Howard Frodsham, *Smith Wigglesworth, Apostle of Faith* (Springfield, MO: Gospel Publishing House, 1948).

Week 18—Day 1
"We Would See Jesus!"

READ LUKE 19:2–6

The church's greatest need today is to look up and see Jesus. The love of many is waxing cold: People are forgetting God, going after pleasure, having a form of godliness and denying the power thereof, denying that Christ baptizes with the Holy Spirit, denying the Virgin Birth of Christ, and denying the efficacy of the blood atonement to save from sin. What a change just one glimpse of the lovely face of Jesus brings!

The world is continuing to creep into the church, and many a place where the fires once kindled upon the altars have long since ceased to burn. Souls are not being saved. Christian hearts are not being set aflame with the glory of the gospel, and the baptism of the Holy Ghost is neither being sought nor desired.

I do not want a little pleasure to keep me from God or from studying the Word, or from prayer. This is the day that we need to see Jesus!

—*Anna D. Britton*
December 1951

Lord, forgive me for allowing a little pleasure and a few distractions to keep me from seeking Your face in prayer. I want to see Jesus! Rekindle any flame that has become dim within me, and increase my hunger and thirst for more of You! Amen.

Bridal Call Foursquare.

Day 2
He's Coming Soon!

READ MATTHEW 25:1–13

Jesus is still the Shepherd, and the sheep that is lost is still you. He hears your cry. Hand over hand, He is coming down, though His hands are torn and His feet are bruised and bleeding. The voice of the Shepherd is calling. Songs of yesterday and of our present day will not live for love, but the song celestial—Jesus Christ—lives forever.

Heed well what I tell you now: It is good news, the best news you have ever heard! He is coming back again! Jesus is coming soon!

We are getting ready, putting oil in our lamps, trimming the wicks, setting fire to them, and waiting and watching for the coming of the gladsome day of our Lord. In the clouds of glory, He is coming for His own:

He's coming, coming soon, I know.
Coming back to this earth to reign,
And the weary pilgrim will to Glory go,
When Jesus comes again.

—Anna D. Britton
December 1931

Lord, I acknowledge my need for You as my Shepherd. Guide and protect me, and prepare me to meet You on the glorious day of Your return. In Your precious name. Amen.

Bridal Call Foursquare.

Day 3

Spiritual Fruit

READ PROVERBS 16:32; JOHN 4:24; GALATIANS 2:20

If our spirit is yielded up to God and He has control of it, there will be peace and joy, a calm amidst all the perplexities and temptations that assail the outward consciousness, or sense-life.

We find our true life, which is Christ. This brings calm to our whole nervous system, and so affects the body, and "the joy of the Lord becomes our strength." Our spirit is the citadel of our whole being. We have perfect control of it; we can use it for our selfish ends, or we can yield it to be possessed by God, or we can, alas, let the adversary control it. It is our free will.

The spirit is a great mystery. It is the part of us that alone can touch the unseen, the unfelt—in short, God and the things of God. Therefore, we only truly live by faith when we learn to live in the Spirit, pray in the Spirit, walk in the Spirit. Then only will the fruit of the Spirit be brought forth, for it is His life, not ours, that brings forth fruit.

—*Mary Boddy*
January 1916

Lord, I yield myself—spirit, soul, and body—and ask that You control my goings and comings so that I may walk in peace and joy and produce much fruit for Your kingdom. In Jesus' name. Amen.

Confidence.

Day 4
Before Our Very Eyes!

READ HOSEA 14

Has indifference been making its effort to claim you? Has self-satisfaction been growing upon you? Has the pressure brought a "weariness in well doing?"

What we need is simply a fresh draught at the fountain, the dew of heaven to rest afresh upon the mown grass of our lives. Bright clouds are hanging heavy over heads, weighted down with showers and with times of refreshing from the presence of the Lord. Let the drooping head be lifted up, and let the parched ground receive. Drink in the rain! Then will the mouth be filled with laughter, and the tongue with singing. The path ahead that appeared dusty and wearisome will be seen to be green with fresh, dew-moistened grass. The drying well will be springing up anew with streams of living water.

Let us not look at the darkness that is growing continually deeper; but let us look upon the light that is shining brighter and brighter. Let us look at the works of God.

—*Zelma E. Argue*
July 1922

Lord, refresh me with Your Spirit and take all "weariness of well doing." Thank You that I can drink from the fountain of Your Presence. In Jesus' name. Amen.

Day 5

Faith: A Vital Force

READ 2 TIMOTHY 4

Faith is a vital force possessing itself of God's facts. Faith is a laying hold of the promises of God in such a way as to make that which is provisionally ours, ours in actual possession. Faith expresses itself by action.

How will a living faith in our Lord express itself? There are three directions.

First, in the personal life it will express itself as a constant and persistent seeking to walk in and obey all the will of God. Then, there will be a zealous faithfulness in witnessing to the unbeliever; and among the brethren, the motive to "exhort one another daily, and so much more as we see the day approaching." And last, toward the Lord, there will be a keen edge on our desire for His fellowship, and for His return, "loving His appearing."

These points are exactly where this spiritual drowsiness would attack the waiting children of the Lord. Here, constant alertness is needed to resist an encroaching lethargy.

—*Zelma E. Argue*
July 1922

Lord, keep my faith vital and cause me to use it daily to combat spiritual lethargy. In Jesus' name. Amen.

The Pentecostal Evangel.

Weekend
Waiting Upon the Lord

READ PSALM 62:5; 130:5-6; ISAIAH 40:31; JOHN 1:1-3

As we wait upon the Lord, there is a change, or passing on, of strength. If we wait upon the Lord, we shall exchange our weakness for His strength. *Exchange* is a better translation of the Hebrew word *chalaph*, meaning "to change, to pass on," than *renew*, as used in Isaiah, chapter 40, the basis for this message.)

As we wait upon the Lord and commune with Him in prayer, we begin to absorb some of His strength. He impresses Himself and His mind upon us. That is why the psalmist says, "My soul, wait thou only upon God; for my expectation is from Him."

—Roxanne Brandt
1973

> Lord, thank You that as I wait on You in prayer, You are faithful to renew my strength. I praise You that for my weakness, You exchange Your strength. My expectation is from You. Amen.

Ministering to the Lord (Springdale, PA: Whitaker House, 1973).

Week 19—Day 1

Absolute Perfection

READ EPHESIANS 5:15–21; COLOSSIANS 3:16–17

Something happened when I was in my teens in Joliet, Illinois. I was preaching the new birth, because that's all I knew. I gave an altar call and some came down. However, a young woman—a teacher—lingered at the altar, praying. Then she, who had never heard someone speak in unknown tongues, raised her hands up and began to sing the most beautiful song I had ever heard. It was absolute perfection!

Her mother grabbed my hand and said, "That is not my daughter, for she can't even carry a note!" We sat there in awe, while the glory was on her face, and it was marvelous. I was learning and seeing the Holy Spirit, witnessing something I hadn't known before. I had seen one baptized in the Holy Spirit.

There is an experience when He fills that vessel of yours. When the Holy Spirit does it, it's absolute perfection. *Jesus Christ* is absolute perfection! This mighty *third Person of the trinity* is absolute perfection! When He speaks through us in unknown tongues, it is *absolute perfection.*

—*Kathryn Kuhlman*
n.d.

Lord, thank You for the absolute perfection of the Holy Spirit's baptism. Fill me fresh each day with Your Spirit. In Jesus' name. Amen.

Condensed and adapted from a chapel service at Oral Roberts University.

Day 2

Brokenness

READ PSALM 34; MARK 6:33–44

People despise brokenness. Psychologists tell us that weeping is a sign of weakness. Well, hallelujah! "When we are weak then we are strong." It is a sign of weakness in the natural man, a weakness of the fleshly, the human. The flesh is altogether weak. Would to God that we knew how weak we really are! We think we can do things for God. We think we can carry on meetings. We think we can put this thing over. That is what *we* think!

But when we get a true vision of our weakness and nothingness and helplessness, we cry to God for help: "O God, I cannot!" And out of that attitude of nothingness and brokenness and humility will come divine strength.

When we bring our all to the Lord to be broken, He accepts the gift. The little lad brought five little cakes—all that he had in his basket. I saw their size when I was once in Palestine—tiny little cakes just six inches in diameter. Jesus took them, broke them, and they became a satisfying portion to five thousand.

—*Hattie Hammond*
March 1938

> *Lord, I accept my brokenness as I acknowledge before You that without You, I am totally weak and entirely helpless. Be my strength and use my brokenness to multiply Your kingdom. In Jesus' name. Amen.*

The Pentecostal Evangel.

Day 3

Broken in His Hands

READ PSALM 51:17; 147:3; EZEKIEL 34:16

It is not what good preachers we are; it is not how well we can sing; the thing that counts is that broken thing that is in His hands, that has His touch upon it, through which He can minister. It will be a satisfying portion. The Holy Ghost will take it and minister it to every heart. He will make the Word that you give forth the message of life to that poor sinner, of comfort to that discouraged one, of healing to that sick one.

—*Hattie Hammond*
March 1938

Lord, take my brokenness and use the gifts You have touched to be a satisfying portion as You pour Your Spirit through me. In Jesus' name. Amen.

The Pentecostal Evangel.

Day 4
Do Not Despise Brokenness

READ PSALM 126:5; EZEKIEL 34:27

The world may despise brokenness, but remember—we are not of this world. God will take the weak ones. If weeping is a sign of weakness, God help us to weep!

In a meeting not long ago a girl came to the altar and began to cry. As she wiped her tears she said, "Oh, pardon me; I did not mean to cry! I know it is a sign of weakness, but really I am not weak. It has been a long time since I cried. Will you forgive me?" I said, "Dear one, for God's sake, weep! Let the tears roll. Let God break through into your inner life and crush you and give you a vision of the Lamb of God, broken and bleeding and hanging on the cross, pouring out His blood to save you from your sins." She broke, and God met her.

True brokenness is such a rare thing that folks have not learned to appreciate it. Folks say, "I do not like these weeping ministers, especially these weeping women!" But if you open your heart, and break with those that are broken, and weep with those who weep, fresh bread will be ministered to you.

—Hattie Hammond
March 1938

Lord, teach me what the Word says about brokenness, and help me to not despise it. As I weep before You, use the tears to keep me melted before You and reliant on Your strength. In Jesus' name. Amen.

Day 5

The Gift Despised

READ REVELATION 7:17

A minister once confessed to me, "It used to be that I could not preach without crying. I saw other ministers did not do it, and one day I said, 'God, why is it that I always have to bawl like a baby every time I am on the platform? Why cannot I be like other people? Why cannot I preach like other men?'"

With tears of confession streaming down his face, he looked at me and said, "Sister, I despised that thing God had given me. I did not appreciate it. When I despised it and complained, God took it away. But today I would give my right arm to get that thing back in my life again!"

—*Hattie Hammond*
March 1938

Lord, forgive me for ever despising tears or viewing them as a sign of weakness. Thank You for the gift of tears and brokenness. In Jesus' name. Amen.

Weekend

The Mystery of Insufficiency

READ JOHN 3:30; EPHESIANS 2:8–10

Peter was so self-sufficient! Only Jesus knew that if Peter were ever to be of any use to Him, He would have to allow Satan to sift him as wheat. Peter was brought to a place of utter self-despair. *Then* God could use him.

Moses thought he was capable of delivering Israel. He drew his sword one day and started delivering the people; he met an Egyptian and killed him. *No, Moses—not that way!* God had to break Moses. Forty years of stern discipline in the wilderness did it. In his brokenness, Moses said, "O God, I cannot talk to Pharaoh!" So God sent Aaron along. *Now* God could use Moses in all his weakness, brokenness, and humility.

The self-sufficient, self-complacent will not appreciate this. Nor will the religious promoter and the creatively energetic whose works and activities are the product of a soulish nature. "Knowledge puffeth up," and those who minister in this realm become hard, boastful, egotistical. But out of the *broken* life there is a flow that brings forth the fullness of Christ.

—Hattie Hammond
March 1938

> *Father, for all Your mercy to me, here is my offering: a broken heart and a contrite spirit—the offering that You will never despise. In Jesus' name. Amen.*

The Pentecostal Evangel.

Week 20—Day 1
We Are Temples

Read 1 Corinthians 3:16–17; 6:19–20; 2 Corinthians 6:16–18

The Bible says that our bodies are the temples of the Holy Spirit. You know what occurred in the temple— praise and worship . . . hours and hours of praise and worship. When we are filled with the Holy Spirit, hours of praise and worship should be poured out to God upon the altars of our hearts. And don't forget—the fire on the altar of the tabernacle in the Old Testament never went out, night or day. Neither does the fire of the Holy Spirit go out in your heart. He burns continually, inspiring you to praise and worship God without ceasing, inspiring you to minister to Him.

That means we minister to Him always. That means at seven o'clock in the morning, when you ladies are turning the eggs over in the frying pan, offer up some spiritual sacrifices unto God. Twenty-four hours a day, whether you are awake or asleep, the Holy Spirit is alive and burning in you. He never goes to sleep. He can use you to minister God.

—Roxanne Brandt
1973

> Lord, thank You for filling me with the Holy Spirit. I am Your temple! Use me in praise and worship, night or day. In Jesus' name. Amen.

Ministering to the Lord (Springdale, PA: Whitaker House, 1973).

Day 2
Prepare Yourself

READ 1 SAMUEL 1:27–28; REVELATION 5:12

We must prepare ourselves to worship the Lord. We cannot turn the television off one minute, and worship the Lord the next minute! We must come apart from noisy, bustling people and situations and still our minds in preparation for worship. We need a place where, individually or collectively, our minds and spirits can be centered on God without distraction.

Abraham came apart to offer up Isaac to God, and he called it worship. To worship means to give something to God, for He is worthy "to receive power, and riches, and wisdom, and strength, and honor, and glory, and blessing" (Rev. 5:12).

The key to worship is to *give something* to God.

—*Roxanne Brandt*
1973

Lord, I prepare myself to worship You by quieting my soul and turning away from all distractions. Help me to offer up myself—my time, my praises—in sacrificial worship to You, holding nothing back. In Jesus' name. Amen.

Ministering to the Lord (Springdale, PA: Whitaker House, 1973).

Day 3
Surrendered to God's Will

READ HEBREWS 11

I was in Finland when a busload of young people were preparing to go to Albania to minister. "Albania?" I said. "That's the only country on earth that has boasted that it has gotten rid of God!" They had closed the last church in Albania and boasted, "At last we're rid of God!" These young people were going over there, and I asked them, "What can you do? You can't preach, you can't pass out tracts. What are you going to do?"

I was told that they would sing. "Nowhere does it say we can't do that!" They said they would drive their bus up one street and down the other, singing—singing at the top of their voices.

"Do you realize you may not come back?" I warned. I'll never forget their reply. One young man, who seemed to be their leader, stood up boldly and said, "Sister, we are prepared for this! We're prepared not to come back. If we don't come back, that's all right. We're surrendered to death!"

—*Hattie Hammond*
n.d.

Lord, prepare me for complete surrender before You!
In Jesus' name. Amen.

Audiocassette titled "Life Bearers," from a chapel service at Christ for the Nations.

Day 4

Two Mothers in Israel

READ TITUS 2:3–5

During the early years of the Pentecostal movement, God raised up hundreds of women to start prayer bands, which later became churches. After these churches were able to obtain pastors, the role of these women changed to that of "spiritual mothers," discipling young women. Thus, the name "mothers in Israel" was conceived.

Mother Garnes had received the baptism of the Holy Spirit in 1902 in the State of Maine. Mother Anderson had received the same baptism in West Virginia. Both moved to Hagerstown, Maryland, where they met at the local Methodist church. After years of praying, they held a tent meeting in 1919, calling in an evangelist for special services. People came from the surrounding area and were saved and baptized in the Holy Spirit. Shortly after the meetings, a pastor was secured—Ralph Jeffrey. When he could not be at all services, Mother Anderson took over. Thus, the newly formed Bethel Assembly of God was birthed by the efforts of two mothers in Israel. These two ladies continued for many decades until their deaths, being role models for many new converts—including Hattie Hammond, the "girl evangelist."

—A historical tribute
n.d.

Lord, use me to guide and disciple younger women in the ways of Your Spirit. In Jesus' name. Amen.

Day 5
The Role of Women

READ JUDGES 4–5; LUKE 8:1–3; GALATIANS 3:28

If a woman's disobedience resulted in the Fall of the human race, let us not forget that it was a woman's obedience that resulted in the redemption.

God chose a woman as His channel for redemption, forgiveness, and eternal salvation. A woman was used to bring joy, peace, love, comfort, and fulfillment to the human race.

Women were active in the ministry of Jesus. The last person at the cross was a woman. The first person at the tomb was a woman. The first person to proclaim the message of the Resurrection was a woman. The first preacher to the Jews was a woman. Women were at the historic prayer meeting following Christ's ascension. Women were in the upper room on the Day of Pentecost, and were given power to be witnesses of Christ. The first persons to greet the Christian missionaries, Paul and Silas, were women. The first European convert was a woman.

—*Daisy Washburn Osborn*
1991

Lord, forgive me for taking for granted the sacrifices women of faith have made throughout history to serve You. Thank You for their lives. Use me, too, to bring You glory. In Jesus' name. Amen.

Women and Self-Esteem (Tulsa, OK: OSFO Publishers, 1991).

Weekend

Comfort for the Sick

READ MARK 16:15–18; JAMES 5:15

Study these texts prayerfully:

- I am the Lord that healeth thee (Exod. 15:26).

- And ye shall serve the LORD your God, and he shall bless thy bread, and thy water; and I will take sickness away from the midst of thee (Exod. 23:25).

- And the Lord will take away from thee all sickness, and will put none of the evil diseases of Egypt, which thou knowest, upon thee (Deut. 7:15).

- Bless the Lord, O my soul: and forget not all His benefits: who forgiveth all thine iniquities; who healeth all thy diseases; who redeemeth thy life from destruction . . . so that thy youth is renewed like the eagle's (Ps. 103:2–5).

- With His stripes we are healed (Isa. 53:5).

- Himself took our infirmities, and bare our sicknesses (Matt. 8:17).

—*Carrie Judd Montgomery*
n.d.

Father, thank You for Your many promises to heal me. Heal me, in Jesus' name, of anything that is wounded or sick or broken within me. I claim Your healing now. In Jesus' name. Amen.

Triumphs of Faith.

Week 21—Day 1

Discouragement

READ 1 SAMUEL 30:1–19

*O*ne of the greatest hindrances to encounter is discouragement. Difficulties can be surmounted; enemies can be overcome; trials can be endured. But when people get discouraged, the sinews of their strength are cut, and the slightest hindrances bar their way and prevent them from going forward.

Many have utterly failed in the great battle of life because they have been discouraged. The Christian has encountered difficulties and adversaries, all of which might have been overcome had the person been of good courage. But the Christian became discouraged, thought he could do nothing, and consequently did nothing.

God calls His servants to be bold and strong. He would not have them faint-hearted or despondent. He knows their weaknesses and frailties. He demands no impossibilities, but He asks that we do our best, that we do not abandon the field or flee through cowardice or despondency. He expects us to trust His promise of help, and He has declared that He will never leave us.

—*Mrs. C. Nuzum*
n.d.

Lord, thank You for encouraging me today against despondency. I trust You to fulfill Your plan for me in Your time—not mine, so increase my faith and patience as I wait on You. Amen.

Triumphs of Faith.

Day 2
The Earnest

READ 2 CORINTHIANS 1:19–22; EPHESIANS 1:1–14

What is an *earnest*? It is just a little handful of a thing—the same quality, but not the quantity. So we can have a little handful here and now of what is going to be ours in eternity. The Holy Spirit is that *earnest* paid on our eternal inheritance.

—*Carrie Judd Montgomery*
May 1942

Lord, thank You for the earnest of the Holy Spirit. Fill me to overflowing with a measure of what will be mine without measure, eternally. In Jesus' name. Amen.

"The Healing Waters," *Triumphs of Faith.*

Day 3
Through Many Waters

READ EZEKIEL 47:1–12

At first the waters were only ankle deep, and then they were knee deep, and then to the loins, and at last "the waters were risen," waters to swim in, a river that could not be passed over. These waters are a symbol of the Holy Ghost. As long as the waters can be measured, you are not in the fullness. You and I have had blessed experiences in the past, and we gave them names, because they could be measured. They were precious experiences, and we were in the river.

But the river kept rising and we went on with our Guide, and finally we came to a place where the rivers were risen and could not be measured. It is lovely to get there, and then we do not talk so much about our experiences as we talk of Jesus. When our feet are no longer on the bottom, we stop measuring and naming our experiences.

Do not stop, beloved, until you reach that place of the fullness of the Spirit, where you are abundantly satisfied, and where you find the waters risen to swim in.

—*Carrie Judd Montgomery*
May 1942

Lord, lead me to the deeps, where I can swim! In Jesus'
name. Amen.

"The Healing Waters," *Triumphs of Faith.*

Day 4
Love Perfected

READ 1 JOHN 4:12

Deep calleth unto deep.
The love of God within my heart of hearts
Calls out to love Divine within thy breast;
His mighty waves and billows o'er us roll.
And in His love we know His perfect rest;
Deep calleth unto deep.

Deep calleth unto deep.
Still deep, deeper yet, we sink in God,
And sinking into Him we sink in love.
Who dwells in Love, dwells also in His God,
And knowing Him we know His heaven above;
Deep calleth unto deep.

Deep calleth unto deep.
So deep we sink, our souls are overflowed
By fullness of His love beyond our ken.
We feel the throbbings of that Heart Divine
Which broke in love upon the hearts of men;
Deep calleth unto deep.

—Carrie Judd Montgomery
May 1942

Lord, I desire to rest in You to the point of sinking—
losing my self-life in service to You, where love is
perfected. In Jesus' name. Amen.

Triumphs of Faith.

Day 5
Force a Fish to Swim?

READ JOHN 4

It is not necessary to frame a law to force a fish to swim in the clear, cool water, or to enjoin him from walking on the dusty highway. Something stronger than any law—life, the fish life—is there, and by virtue of it, he swims happily in the crystal stream.

You don't have to legislate to make an eagle spurn the earth and soar heavenward; the eagle life is there. And you don't have to try and try to be holy and whole, sound spiritually and physically. It doesn't come that way. Trying gets you back under the law of fleshly commandment. It is by receiving the all-conquering life of the risen Christ that it is to be accomplished. Receive Him, the Resurrection and the Life, by faith. Then your life no longer flows from your natural constitution, inherited from your parents, but from your risen Lord.

—*Dr. Lillian B. Yeomans*
June 1930

Lord, thank You that because I have received You, Your life flows into me as the natural outflowing of the Holy Spirit. Keep me filled to the brim. In Jesus' name. Amen.

"Resurrection Rays," *The Pentecostal Evangel.*

Weekend

Living Waters

READ JEREMIAH 2:13; 17:13–14; JOHN 7:37–38

We need to turn to God and let Him, the Fountain of Life-Giving Waters, flow through us, cleanse us, and fill us daily with His life. We need to have God, by His Spirit, reveal things to us in a fresh way. We need to go to God for Himself, and for a Living Word.

The Pharisees knew what God had said. They had built cisterns. They were opaque and deaf to what God was saying in their time, simply because they had forsaken Him and built little cisterns around His Word. We need to know what God has said and what He is saying today. When we, like the Pharisees of old, are not in God's life-giving flow, then our spiritual senses tend to become dulled and deadened. Then we have little or no spiritual perception and discernment.

God cries, "Come unto Me!" Then we will be satisfied with the life-giving words of God.

—*Roxanne Brandt*
1973

Father, thank You for Your living Word; its waters provide cleansing and healing and revelation. Forgive me if in any way I have built cisterns against the flow. Break them open, Lord, and send a mighty flood! In Jesus' name. Amen.

Ministering to the Lord (Springdale, PA: Whitaker House, 1973).

Week 22—Day 1

Troublemaker or Peacemaker?

READ HEBREWS 1:8–9

There was a boy who whined and grumbled every time he was asked to do anything. He got mad at his top because it didn't spin right. He was so quarrelsome over a game he was playing with some boys that he got all the other boys quarreling too. If you were giving that boy a name, what would you call him? How would Tommy Troublemaker suit?

There is also the story of a boy who carried a little can of oil with him everywhere he went, and if he passed through a door that squeaked, he poured a little oil on the hinges. If he came to a gate and it opened hard, he oiled it. And so he passed through life, oiling all the rusty, squeaky hard places, and making it easier for those who came after him. He filled his can daily and carried it with him to oil. If you were to give that boy a name, what would you call him? How would Paul Peacemaker suit?

Jesus said, "Blessed are the peacemakers, for they shall be called the children of God."

—*Sister Beulah*
February 1925

> *Lord, please make me a peacemaker, not a trouble-*
> *maker; fill me with Your oil daily so that I can be used*
> *to ease the way for those who come after me. In Jesus'*
> *name. Amen.*

"The Children's Corner," *The Pentecostal Evangel*

Day 2
A Word to Mothers

READ DEUTERONOMY 6:4–9; PROVERBS 31:10–31

Mother, it is your blessed privilege to lead your own children to the Lord Jesus. I am so glad the Lord gave me the sweet joy of being alone with my little daughter when she was saved and when she received the baptism in the Holy Spirit. No greater joy can come to a mother's heart.

This is a wicked and sinful world, and our children are not safe outside of Jesus Christ. Let us spend much time in prayer for our dear ones that they may all be brought into the fold and made ready for the coming Jesus. It is God's will to save whole families. He said to Noah, "Come thou and all thy house into the ark." The Tribulation days are almost upon us. God grant that before the dark night falls upon this godless, unbelieving earth, all our loved ones may be safe in the Everlasting Arms.

—*Mae Eleanor Frey*
June 1921

Lord, grant me the privilege of leading my children to You. Give me the words and the wisdom to model Christ at all times in our home. I lift my children to You now, and claim their souls for Christ. In Jesus' name. Amen.

The Pentecostal Evangel.

Day 3

Three Girls Start a Revival

READ ISAIAH 11:6; MATTHEW 18:2–6

Annie Sinclair, Christy Campbell, and Christy Anderson—aged from ten to twelve—began a midday prayer meeting back of the schoolhouse. From the very first this little prayer meeting was of great power. Boys and girls were converted, the first convert being a lad of ten.

The prayer meeting grew in numbers and in power. The pastor became interested. From the woods the meeting was taken to the parsonage, and then to the church. Soon the church was filled to overflowing with anxious souls seeking salvation. The people came from many miles, and there was a genuine revival. The wonderful revival continued for nearly two years, until hundreds were converted, and the entire face of the country was changed. Out of that revival came foreign missionaries, ministers, college professors, Sunday school superintendents and teachers, church workers in all ranks of life. It came about in answer to the prayers of three little girls. No one can tell until the books are opened what wonderful results flowed from those prayer meetings! If three little girls could do that, why can't you?

—*Unknown*
n.d.

*Lord, use me . . . use my children to light revival fires
and to lead others to Christ. In Jesus' name. Amen.*

"Young Folks' Department," *Word and Work.*

Day 4
Hiding From God

READ 1 SAMUEL 16:7; 1 JOHN 3:18–24

A teacher once held up a vase of water in which a goldfish was swimming about, and said to the children, "See this fish hide! Do you see him now?"

"Yes, sir," the children shouted.

And as the fish moved in all directions, the teacher asked, "Do you see him now?" It brought the same eager reply: "Yes, sir!"

"Can't he hide from you?" asked the teacher.

"No, sir," was the reply.

"Why?"

"Because we see through the glass."

"So," said the teacher, "God sees right through our hearts. We cannot hide from Him."

—Unknown
August 1920

Lord, I repent of ever trying to hide from You! You see right into my heart at all times. Purify my heart so that I may never fear that fact. In Jesus' name. Amen.

"Young Folks' Department," *Word and Work.*

Day 5

Raised From Death

READ MARK 5:22–42

My little Virginia, opening the wrong door, fell down the stairway to the concrete floor of a deep cellar. Her face was so bruised as to make her countenance unrecognizable. Her chin and forehead were mashed in and her nose mashed flat. When I picked her up, those nearby cried, "She is dead! Her neck is broken!"

I carried her up the stairs and laid her on the couch. Feeling her pulse, I could feel no life. Some wanted to call a doctor. I had been a nurse, and knowing that she was already dead, told them that a doctor could do her no good. But I held on to the Lord in prayer for her. And, praise His name, after she had lain that way for an hour with no sign of life, she opened her eyes and spoke, saying, "Satan is defeated. Jesus has healed me."

Little Virginia was only seven years old and knew nothing of the working of the Lord. Just then the power of God came on her. Her features became normal. Then she said, "Jesus, my beloved Jesus, has healed me. Everybody get down and pray."

—*Gussie Booth*
n.d.

Lord, thank You that resurrection power resides in You! I praise You for what You have done to raise little Virginia from death—and that what You have done, You will do again! In Jesus' name. Amen.

"Little Girl Raised From Death," *Triumphs of Faith.*

Weekend
"God Don't Make No Dummies!"

READ EPHESIANS 2:4–10

There was a five-year-old boy who, on his first day in kindergarten, was asked by his teacher to tell something about himself. The boy obviously came from a loving home and had good seeds sown in him. He told his name and then added self-confidently:

"I'm good, 'cause God don't make nothin' bad. I'm handsome, 'cause God don't make nothin' ugly. And I'm smart, 'cause God don't make no dummies."

What a dynamic and simple acceptance of a God-inspired, God-created, individualized human person! That lad said it all in a nutshell. His was a good self-image—a positive esteem.

Can you be as honest and as forthright as that five-year-old boy? Always remember that you are God's idea. That means you are a very special creation—not the result of an assembly line of robots. You have a unique purpose in God's plan.

—*Daisy Washburn Osborn*
1986

Father, thank You for creating me to be unique, one of a kind. Fill me with confidence about that fact as I worship You as Creator and give You glory for my uniqueness. In Jesus' name. Amen.

5 *Choices for Women Who Win* (Tulsa, OK: OSFO Publishers, 1986).

Week 23—Day 1

Broken Cisterns

READ MARK 11:22–24; JOHN 14:13–14; 1 JOHN 5:14–15

God amazed me several years ago when He showed me that many people involved in the Charismatic movement had turned to "broken cisterns" instead of to Him. Because of the abundant outpouring of good teaching, people were purchasing tapes and books and attending seminars to learn more about God's power and His ways and what He was doing on earth at that time. Tapes and books and conferences are good! In fact, you're reading a book right now that hopefully will encourage you as you seek to draw more closely to God.)

But the Lord showed me that His people were substituting other sources for spending time in prayer, waiting on Him. Sometimes it is so easy to hear from others *about* God and what He is doing that we don't bother to come to Him to find out *what He wants to say to us*. We don't bother to commune with Him and receive the life-giving Word for ourselves. Then we draw from broken cisterns. And the water from cisterns is never as fresh and pure as the water from God's moving, flowing, life-giving fountain.

—*Roxanne Brandt*
1973

Lord, thank You for the books and tapes and seminars that You have enriched me through, but help me always to seek You first. In Jesus' name. Amen.

Ministering to the Lord (Springdale, PA: Whitaker House, 1973).

Day 2
The Day You Eat . . .

READ DEUTERONOMY 30:19–20; JOSHUA 24:14–15

When Adam sinned, the whole human race went into eclipse, darkness, and death. Adam didn't fall; Adam died! God had said to him of the forbidden fruit, "The day you eat, you'll die!" This has been God's message straight through the Book: Choose life or death.

There are still two trees in the garden. If you eat of the right tree you'll live, if you eat of the wrong tree you'll die. Adam didn't realize what he was getting himself into; he had never seen anything dead in his life. He had never seen a dead tree, a dead leaf, a dead blade of grass. He had never seen a dead bird, a dead flower, and had no knowledge of what sin could do.

Sin is a terrible thing! Hate it with everything that's in you. Don't have anything to do with it, for the day you eat, you'll die!

—*Hattie Hammond*
n.d.

Lord, give me wisdom and discernment to always eat of the right tree—the Tree of Life! In Jesus' name. Amen.

Audiocassette titled "Life Bearers," from a chapel service at Christ for the Nations.

Day 3
Choose God

READ PHILIPPIANS 1:21–30

God created every woman with a will. We are constantly exercising that will. God never violates our will or our choices, but He guides us in His way of success as we allow His Word to keep us tuned to His wavelength. We may even make a bad choice, but He never gives up on us, because He has given us the power to make another choice to correct the bad one.

When you choose Jesus, then you are free from Satan's power and he is no longer your master. You are no longer his slave. Jesus becomes your Lord, your Leader, and your Master. You become His servant; you become His physical expression on this earth.

You can serve only one master, and the choice of masters is the right of every woman to make.

—*Daisy Washburn Osborn*
1991

Lord, I choose You! Guide me to fulfill Your perfect plan for my life. In Jesus' name. Amen.

Women and Self-Esteem (Tulsa, OK: OSFO Publishers, 1991).

Day 4
The Secret of Revival

READ 2 CHRONICLES 7:12–18

"What is the secret of revival?" a great revivalist was asked. "There is no secret," he replied. "Revival always comes in answer to prayer."

Before America can have a sweeping, Holy Ghost revival, there must be a revival of prayer. And before this revival of prayer can come, there must be a conviction of sin and an open confession of the same among all followers of Christ. All movements of the Spirit in the past, without exception, have been started as the initial outpouring upon the hundred and twenty in the upper room—by the force of intense, believing prayer. Whenever the early church prayed as related in the Book of Acts, we find the Spirit miraculously poured out.

The Weslyan Revival, like Pentecost, came in answer to persistent, prevailing prayer. The practice of the primitive Methodists was to pray from four to five o'clock in the morning, religiously, and from five to six o'clock every evening. The leaders and founders of Methodism, themselves, spent hours and even all night in an agony of importunate prayer, and started revival fires wherever they preached the Word.

—*Sarah Foulkes Moore*
July 1941

Lord, I give myself to You in prayer; use me to help pray in the next great revival! Amen.

"God's Plan for Setting the World Aflame," *The Pentecostal Evangel.*

Day 5

Birthed in Prayer

READ ACTS 12:5–16

In Wales before the Great Revival at the opening of the twentieth century, three hundred extra praying bands were formed. It was as though Wales had become one great prayer meeting. In 1903, the churches of Wales were empty, and vice was rampant. In 1904, Wales was swept by a mighty Holy Ghost revival, the churches were filled to overflowing, and within two months seventy thousand souls found Jesus Christ!

—*Sarah Foulkes Moore*
July 1941

Lord, thank You for the fire of the Holy Ghost—fire fanned in prayer and about to set the world aflame for Christ! Amen.

"God's Plan for Setting the World Aflame," *The Pentecostal Evangel.*

Weekend
Revival Fires Spread

READ JAMES 5:13–18

In Calcutta, India, Dr. R. A. Torrey addressed a group of missionaries. Two of the ladies present were so impressed with the importance he placed upon intense, believing prayer, that they returned to their mission station and prevailed upon their people to seek the Lord in prayer. Soon a great many in the district were on their knees, crying out to God. Revival was inevitable, and within a short time eight thousand souls were saved.

Hearing of the marvelous story of India's revival, missionaries in Korea decided to pray every day until a similar revival was poured out on them. "After we had prayed for about a month," said one of the missionaries, "a brother proposed that we stop . . . The majority of us, however, decided that instead . . . we would give *more* time to prayer, not less. We changed the hour from noon to four o'clock in the morning. We kept at it until at last after several months, the answer came." And what an answer! Over five hundred thousand Koreans were swept into the kingdom on the flood tide of this revival!

—*Sarah Foulkes Moore*
July 1941

Father, fan the flames of world revival through my prayers. Direct my prayers, by the power of the Spirit. In Jesus' name. Amen.

"God's Plan for Setting the World Aflame," *The Pentecostal Evangel*.

Week 24—Day 1
Will to Pray

READ MATTHEW 6:1–8

When you really "will to pray," find a closet and enter in—and pray. Don't just say prayers; pray! Your will enters into this thing. If you really will to pray and get through to God in prayer, the minute you say it, all hell comes up against you.

Before you can get on your knees, the telephone rings. Before you can begin, the devil attacks your mind with suggestions: "You ought to do this," or, "You ought to do that!" "You'd better take care of this right now!" All that's pure devil!

There have been times when I have had to stomp my foot and say, "Devil, go to hell where you belong!" That's strong language, but you have to treat the devil like the devil—especially when your will is to pray!

—*Hattie Hammond*
n.d.

Lord, thank You that I have been given power over the enemy by Jesus Christ at Calvary. Help me to discern the devil's wiles, especially his attempts to keep me from praying. Help me to resist the devil, and pray! In Jesus' name. Amen.

Audiocassette titled "How to Pray," from a chapel service at Christ for the Nations.

Day 2
True and False Prophets

READ 2 PETER 2

When you hear the Word and you are motivated and living it out, then the Spirit of Truth is operating in you. However, if you say that you are this and that, and the Word is not performing, happening, or working in you, then you are liable to be in the spirit of error. It is not enough to say it, but we must have the operation of the Spirit of Truth in our lives. It is a necessity.

Jesus, not man, is the true prophet. It is Jesus operating through the one who occupies the office of a prophet. False prophets want recognition. They want to exercise authority instead of responsibility. The people who are the most anointed of God are the least likely to parade it around.

False prophets deal with the external instead of the internal things of the heart. A true prophet knows how to balance his public ministry and private devotion. A good tree will bear the fruit of the Spirit—which is love, joy, peace, patience, goodness, meekness, faithfulness, gentleness, and self-control.

— *Jeanne Wilkerson*
n.d.

Lord, give me the discernment to distinguish between true and false prophets. Help me to use the test of "fruit inspection," along with the plumbline of Your Word, to tell the difference. Amen.

Audiocassette titled "How to Know True and False Prophets."

Day 3

Christ Reaching Out

READ MATTHEW 25:34–46

The only way Christ can reach out His arms and lay His divine hands of blessing on lives is through you. You are His body now. His ministry in your community is expressed through you as a woman. He longs to speak to people about their salvation. He longs to convince them of the gospel. He can do it through you.

He wants to visit the lost, the sick, and the prisoners, and to bless them. Now He can do it through you. It is your mission as a woman. He will never send angels to do His work. He operates through you now. If you are too busy with other things or if you think you are not good enough, or if you feel that your own affairs are more important, or if you think you do not have time, then your Christ is like a statue: He has no hands.

—*Daisy Washburn Osborn*
1991

Lord, I desire to be Your hands! Use me to reach out to those around me. In Jesus' name. Amen.

Women and Self-Esteem (Tulsa, OK: OSFO Publishers, 1991).

Day 4
No Hands but Yours

READ PSALM 90:12–17

During World War II a beautiful statue of Jesus in France was damaged. The villagers there lovingly gathered up the pieces of their statue that had stood in front of their church, and they repaired it. But they never found the hands.

Some of the people said, "What good is our Christ without hands?"

That gave someone else an idea, and he had a bronze plaque attached to the statue, engraved with these words: *I have no hands but your hands!*

—*Daisy Washburn Osborn*
1991

Lord, I give You my hands: Use them! In Jesus' name.
Amen.

Women and Self-Esteem (Tulsa, OK: OSFO Publishers, 1991).

Day 5
A Note From My Diary

READ PSALM 24

While waiting on the Lord in the home of Brother and Sister V. God met me in a precious way and began speaking to my heart . . . a little later He asked me if I would enlist for some new thing from Him. Today, October 2, 1927, I enroll in the Book of my Lord for some new thing from Him: "A reckless adventure in Jesus Christ!" The things required are a pure mind, clean thoughts, holy heart, yielded life, unbroken communion with a sanctified prayer life—not paying attention to the devil, but without ceasing, praising God for victory.

—*Hattie Hammond*
October 1927

Lord, I too enroll in Your Book for a "reckless adventure in Jesus Christ!" Sign me up! Purify me, filling me with Your praises and the unmistakable knowledge of my victory in Christ. In Jesus' name. Amen.

Excerpted from Hattie Hammond's diary.

Weekend
Jottings

READ JOHN 14

From sermon notes:

When Christ came to earth He found man *dissatisfied* with his circumstances and *satisfied* with himself.

When He left the earth He left man *dissatisfied* with himself and *satisfied* with his surroundings.

When Christ came to earth man valued the *world* above everything and his *soul* as nothing.

When Christ left the earth man valued his *soul* above everything and the *world* as nothing.

When Christ came to earth He found the world as *servants* wanting to be *masters*.

When He left the earth the world was *masters* wanting to be *servants*.

—Hattie Hammond
October 1927

Father, thank You for what Jesus did; He turned the world upside down—or should I say, right side up! Thank You for setting things right for me—for all mankind! Amen.

Excerpted from Hattie Hammond's diary.

Week 25—Day 1
Preach, Pray, and Prophesy

READ JOEL 2:28; 1 CORINTHIANS 11:5; 14:3

I must truthfully say that I have found no scripture forbidding a woman to preach, pray, or prophesy. Instead, I found a large number of permission scriptures. The words *preach* and *prophesy* cannot be separated. "But he that prophesieth speaketh unto men to edification, and exhortation, and comfort." That is exactly what a preacher does. The word *prophesy* means "to speak, or foretell, under divine influence."

In the Book of Joel, God said that women would prophesy. Paul the Apostle also stated that women would prophesy. Some say women should not minister to a mixed group. However, we find that Priscilla helped her husband to instruct Apollos more fully in the way of the Lord. See Acts 18–26.) Phoebe, an unmarried woman in the church, attended and took part in a business meeting at Paul's commission. See Romans 16:1–2.) The great letter to the Romans was delivered by her. And women had a prominent part of the ministry of Christ Himself. All four Gospels bear out the fact that after His resurrection Christ appeared first to women. Jesus ordained women to tell the men that He was risen.

—*Juanita Coe*
n.d.

Thank You, Lord, for using women throughout history to proclaim the glorious gospel. Use me as You see fit. In Jesus' name. Amen.

Women Preachers (n.p., n.d.).

Day 2

Simplicity

READ MATTHEW 18:1–6

Simplicity is a very effective tool in breaking the bondage of things. You require nothing to be yourself. What you are does not depend on what you have. A young man tells how humbling it was to him when he discovered that young people were looking to him for leadership. He said, "I must not fail to be what people think I am." I know what that will mean in his life: not the accumulation of things in order to impress people that he is a success, but the study, the prayer, and disciplined living that will result in the type of spiritual character on which people can depend and by which they can be inspired.

Simplicity always functions in that direction. When we are willing to be known for what we are, we do not resort to things to conceal what we are or to convey the impression of greatness to those who are so easily impressed by the gadgets in which our civilization abounds. It is no wonder Jesus said, "Except ye be converted and become as little children, ye shall not enter into the kingdom of heaven."

—Juanita Coe
n.d.

Lord, work simplicity into the fabric of my walk so that I can walk childlike before You, not caring about the opinions of others or the way I appear outwardly. In Jesus' name. Amen.

On Being a Real Christian (n.p., n.d.).

Day 3

God Ordained Marriage

READ GENESIS 2:21–25

God ordained marriage, and everything He created is beautiful. A happy marriage does not come accidentally, and neither does it come overnight. Both partners must make a quality decision to put God's Word first. Marriage is a spiritual contract, a miraculous union. In it, the bride and groom are joined together not only in body and soul, but spiritually as well. A husband and wife form the strongest bond there is between two human beings. The marriage is much more than a man and a woman saying, "I do!" It is a serious relationship in God's eyes and is not to be entered into lightly.

Consistent Christian behavior in the home is the key to a successful marriage. The man and woman must make a decision that the home is going to be a place of refuge, peace, harmony, and beauty. If couples would bring the same planning, the same wisdom, the same assessment into their marriages as they do their businesses, many of our domestic problems would be solved.

—*Leona Sumrall Murphy*
1984

Lord, I submit my marriage to You! Please make me and my mate consistent in the home, and help me to take marriage as the most serious covenant relationship of my life. Bless my marriage, Lord! In Jesus' name. Amen.

Marriage Is a Triangle (South Bend, IN: LeSEA Publishing Co., 1984).

Day 4

Speaking in Tongues

READ ACTS 2:4–21

"So you've been speaking in tongues, have you?" she said somewhat scornfully. In a subdued voice he responded, "Well, er . . . Yes!"

"Well, I want you to understand," his wife said firmly, "I am as much baptized as you are, and I don't speak in tongues!" Then pushing the knife in a little further, she added, "I've been preaching for more than twenty years and you have sat beside me on the platform, tongue-tied. But on Sunday, you'll preach yourself, my man, and I'll see what there is in it!"

That said, Polly walked out of the room, leaving a very thoughtful, and perhaps a little shaken, Smith Wigglesworth.

—*Polly Wigglesworth*
1948

> *Lord, is there anything to this business of tongues? If so, and it's a blessing from You, then send tongues, by the power of Your Spirit. In Jesus' name. Amen.*

Stanley Howard Frodsham, *Smith Wigglesworth: Apostle of Faith* (Springfield, MO: Gospel Publishing House, 1948).

Day 5

"What's Happened to the Man?"

READ ISAIAH 61

*S*mith Wigglesworth walked the length of the hall with a small Bible in his hand, ascended the three short steps to the platform. As he walked toward the front of the hall, he had not known what he would say. But as he ascended the platform, God spoke to him: He was told to begin with Isaiah, chapter 61.

Then he began to preach. Soon he felt the mighty power of God surge through him, and though he had a limited vocabulary, words rushed out of him like a torrent of water. Previously, when he had attempted to preach, he had always broken down weeping; but now he was fluent.

Polly sat in the back of the hall . . . completely astounded. As Smith continued with his preaching, Polly kept moving from one part of the bench to the other, talking to herself: "That's not my Smith! Amazing . . . amazing! *What's happened to the man?*"

—*Polly Wigglesworth*
n.d.

Lord, I too wish to be transformed by the power of the Holy Spirit! Fill me with that same dynamic confidence as you did Smith Wigglesworth. In Jesus' name. Amen.

Stanley Howard Frodsham, *Smith Wigglesworth: Apostle of Faith* (Springfield, MO: Gospel Publishing House, 1948).

Weekend

Unity in Prayer

READ PHILIPPIANS 1

Unity in prayer has turned the tide in national crises, for England is acknowledged by historians to have been saved from a similar bloody revolution as that which swept through France, through the ministry of John Wesley and his associates.

In 1738 Wesley went to a Moravian prayer meeting, where he heard Peter Boler unfolding the Book of Ephesians. Something happened. Later, Wesley wrote: "While Peter Boler taught, I felt my heart strangely warmed, and I could then and there for the first time say assuredly that my sins were forgiven through Jesus Christ my Lord."

That "little Moravian prayer meeting" lasted a hundred years. Bishop Hasse wrote that the great outpouring of the Spirit among the Moravians during the eighteenth century was the greatest since Pentecost. "Was there ever in the whole church history such an astonishing prayer meeting as that which, beginning at Herrnhut in 1727, went on one hundred years?"

—*Sarah Elias Foulkes*
November 1936

Father, give me a heart and the vision for the unity of prayer. Make me a woman of prayer so that You can do great works through me—whether or not I ever get to go "into all the world and preach the gospel." In Jesus' name. Amen.

Week 26—Day 1
The Work of the Lord?

READ MATTHEW 14:23; LUKE 11:1–4; 18:1

So often the work of the Lord suffers while we are busy with the work of the Lord.

We have put our first ministry second. We really need to repent, because in doing that we have committed idolatry. We have exalted the institution of ministry above our Lord. We have exalted the traditions of men above the Lord Himself. We are busy doing this or that or something else. What God is trying to say to us is, "Peace, be still! Go somewhere and minister to Me. Then there will be no wasted efforts, no wasted words, and all will be done in the power of My Spirit."

Some people find it hard to believe, but every time I draw apart, He meets me. Every time! I don't care where it is, it only takes a few minutes before I am caught up in worship to Him. This can happen to you too, if you cultivate your relationship with Him. It takes time and effort, but certainly no one else is as worthy of your full attention as the living God.

—Roxanne Brandt
1973

Lord, forgive me for getting too busy for You! I return to my first love—ministry to You—and ask that You meet me in the secret place of prayer. In Jesus' name. Amen.

Ministering to the Lord (Springdale, PA: Whitaker House, 1973).

Day 2
Because We Love Him

READ LUKE 2:36–37

Anna, the prophetess, spent much time ministering to the Lord and in communion with Him.

I'll be honest; when I first became a Christian, I read that passage in Luke, chapter 2, and decided that Anna had to minister to the Lord with fastings and prayers night and day because she was so old. I assumed that she did not have anything else to do. Or that she could not do anything practical, like bringing people to God, because she was too aged and weak.

Now I realize that she was simply expressing her love for Him. When we come to the Lord for Himself and express our love for Him, His heart is moved. He pours out His blessing upon us and grants our requests in a lavish way.

—*Roxanne Brandt*
1973

Lord, I express my love to You, simply for who You are! I honor You and magnify Your name! Thank You for loving me enough to send Your Son in my stead. I love You, Lord! Amen.

Ministering to the Lord (Springdale, PA: Whitaker House, 1973).

Day 3

Power to Preach Good News

READ MARK 15:15; GALATIANS 3:28–29

God trusts a woman who is saved as much as He trusts a man who is saved, because He believes in His righteousness in one the same as in the other. He has given us the power of His Holy Spirit to enable us to share the Good News effectively. He trusts that we will do it.

Paul wrote, "We are no longer Jews or Greeks or slaves or free men or even merely men or women, but we are all the same—we are Christians: we are one in Christ . . . and all of God's promises . . . belong to us" (TLB). That is for me as a woman as much as it is for T. L. Osborn, a man.

All that God is belongs to all who receive Christ, whether they are men or women.

—*Daisy Washburn Osborn*
1986

Lord, thank You that You have enabled me, by the power of the Holy Spirit, to share the Good News. Help me to do it gladly, and often. Use me to witness. In Jesus' name. Amen.

5 *Choices for Women Who Win* (Tulsa, OK: OSFO Publishers, 1986).

Day 4

The River Flows In and Out

READ JOHN 7:37–39; 1 CORINTHIANS 15:45

We are vehicles through which the life and power of God can flow into this dark world. Jesus is the life, and as we come to Him and drink, that life flows into us. Then, as we praise and worship God, that life flows out of us toward God. As we obey God and move by faith, that life flows through us into the deserts of the world.

When we come to Jesus and drink, an inflow of life is established. God also wants to establish an outflow of life. He does not want us to merely receive life, but to come to the place where He can impart the life of the Holy Spirit through us . . . the place where His life flows out from us to others. He wants to put the same Spirit in us that was in Jesus, so that out of the Holy Spirit can flow rivers of life-giving water.

—*Roxanne Brandt*
1973

Lord, fill me to the brim with Your Spirit, and let it spill over, flowing out as a mighty, life-giving river to those around me. In Jesus' name. Amen.

Ministering to the Lord (Springdale, PA: Whitaker House, 1973).

Day 5
Like Christ

READ MATTHEW 26:27; LUKE 9:56; JOHN 14:10; 1 JOHN 4:17

In a world His hands had made,
Not a place to lay His head!
A partaker let me be
Of His sweet humility.

Nothing owned, and nothing had,
From His Father's hand was fed.
Thus He let me renounce my life,
End of conflict, end of strife.

Miracles on every side,
"The Father's works," thus He cried,
My helplessness here I see
Is God's room to work in me.

Author of all worlds now view!
"Of Myself I nothing do!"
Through me that His works may show,
Empty may I ever go.

On the throne with ceaseless care,
Lives He ever to make prayer:
Seated "with Him," let me plead
All the world's exceeding need.

—*Elizabeth Sisson*
August 1917

Let it be so, Lord. Amen.

The Weekly Evangel.

Weekend

"*It Shall Be Done!*"

READ ROMANS 4:18–21; HEBREWS 11:11; JAMES 4:3

Faith considers absolutely nothing but the promise of God. It laughs at the impossibilities and cries, "It shall be done!" Look at the sublime faith of Rachel: She said, "God shall add to me another son." And God did add another son. Faith is never disappointed.

O dear, disappointed one, have you given up expecting things from God and settled down into the ordinary Christian life? Let us stir ourselves to prayer, as Daniel, and God will surely hear.

Dear one, can God say of you as He did of David, "I have found David a man after My heart who will fulfill My will?" He is seeking such today. His eyes run to and fro throughout the whole earth, to show Himself strong to those whose hearts are perfect toward Him.

—*Margaret Gordon*
August 1917

Lord, purify my heart so that it is turned toward You, to fulfill Your will. Increase my faith so that, regardless of circumstances, I will say, "It shall be done!" Amen.

The Weekly Evangel.

Part 3—
III Summer

. . . a time
to laugh . . .

—Ecclesiastes 3:4, NKJV

Week 27—Day 1
The Dead Sea Will Flourish

READ REVELATION 22:1–5

There is no outflow of water from the Dead Sea. It is dead because there is no outlet. This is true of many people's lives also, and that is why they are spiritually dead.

But God's river is going to run into the Dead Sea, and the waters are going to be healed. There will be an outlet and inflow of the Mediterranean Sea into the Dead Sea, and a very great multitude of fish will come into the Dead Sea.

Since an ocean or a sea in the Bible signifies a mass of humanity, the Dead Sea signifies a mass of spiritually dead humanity. But God is going to cause His increasing swelling River of Life to flow into the great mass of unregenerate humanity. They will drink of that water of life and be healed.

—*Roxanne Brandt*
1973

Lord, heal the waters of those who are spiritually dead,
and use me to reach them! In Jesus' name. Amen.

Ministering to the Lord (Springdale, PA: Whitaker House, 1973).

Day 2

Rivers in the Desert

READ ISAIAH 43:19–20; EZEKIEL 47:1

God is bringing forth "rivers in the desert" and "waters in the wilderness to give drink to His people." As the hungry and thirsty come unto Him and drink, His life will flow into them and they will worship Him in a river of praise.

Then they will move out to obey Him, doing exploits in the power of the Holy Spirit.

Ezekiel saw this increasing, swelling river of God beginning as a little stream and growing into a huge river about three miles wide. That is what is happening to some degree in our time.

—*Roxanne Brandt*
1973

Lord, I want to flow in the River of Life. Fill me with Your praises, let them spill out, and from there, direct me for Your use. In Jesus' name. Amen.

Ministering to the Lord (Springdale, PA: Whitaker House, 1973).

Day 3
Water for the Thirsty

READ JOHN 6:32–38

Did you ever see a thirsty person? Did you ever see a traveler who had walked for miles in the heat of the sun in the summer months? Have you seen them wipe the perspiration from their brow, or how happy they were to get to a fountain of water? Oh, how happy they were to get that drink of water!

The way to tell if a person has natural thirst is to take a glass of water. I could start through a group of people and ask, "How many of you would like to have a drink?" And it wouldn't be long before I would find out who wanted a drink, because they would be reaching out to me.

Today I am offering you living water. If you taste it, you will never thirst again. I am offering you bread; if you eat it, you will never hunger again, because Jesus is the bread of life. If you have not drunk of the water of life, if you have not eaten the bread of life, then you don't know what you have missed.

—Juanita Coe
n.d.

Lord, I drink again of the water of life, and again, I eat the bread of life. I thank You for providing the water and bread that will take away my hunger and thirst for eternity! Amen.

Women Preachers.

Day 4
There Was a Rich Man . . .

READ LUKE 16:20–31

There was a poor beggar named Lazarus who died and was carried to the bosom of Abraham. As he was there, enjoying all the good things God had promised to His children, there was a rich man in hell who lifted up his eyes and said, "Father Abraham, could you send Lazarus to dip his finger in water and touch my tongue? I'm tormented in these flames!"

There is a hell where the flames are not quenched, although some say there isn't. If you do not take God into the plans for your life, you may soon feel those flames. You may cry out, as the rich man did, "Oh, do something for me!" But it will be too late to cry then. The time to cry is now. The rich man died, the Scriptures say, and his riches failed to help him. He may have tried to buy his way out of hell, but no—there is no need for money in heaven where the streets are of gold, the gates are of pearl, and the walls are of jasper.

Don't wait! Turn to God before it is too late.

—*Juanita Coe*
n.d.

Lord, I turn to You as the Author and Finisher of my faith. Thank You for Your mercy, and for the love for me that motivated Jesus to take my sins upon Himself at Calvary. In Jesus' name. Amen.

Women Preachers.

Day 5
Revival Is Coming!

READ JOHN 17

It was a time of spiritual dearth and unfavorable conditions when the great revival of 1857 broke out in New York City. People were so occupied with the affairs of this life that they were not interested in spiritual things.

Nevertheless, God had His praying man—someone who pressed into the Spirit because of the sins of the unrighteous. One single man—a layman, not a minister of the gospel—was so burdened for the people that he called a noonday prayer meeting, and when the time came he went to the appointed place and prayed. For half an hour he prayed alone until others dropped in. Six composed the first prayer meeting.

Interest grew from day to day until other places were opened for prayer throughout the city. As it gathered momentum, nearly every hamlet and community in the nation felt the quickening effect of the prayer meetings, and the influence extended even to other shores. Hundreds of thousands were brought to Christ in what was perhaps the most widespread visitation ever known on this continent.

—Louise Nankivell
December 1944

Lord, stir me up to pray more fervently for global revival. In Jesus' name. Amen.

"Revival Is Coming," *The Pentecostal Evangel*.

Weekend

The Day of the Great Revivals

READ ACTS 2:16–21

We are told that the day of the great revivals is over . . . that we can no longer expect mass revivals with thousands converted. The enemy of our souls would like to have us think so, but this is not true.

God is not willing that any should perish, but that all should come to repentance. There is no reason why we should not yet see one of the greatest spiritual awakenings which has ever come upon the earth! "With God nothing shall be impossible!" "All things are possible to him that believeth!" "Have faith in God."

I believe God for such a great revival; will you?

—*Louise Nankivell*
December 1944

Lord, give me the heart and the vision for global revival; I acknowledge that these are the End Times, and realize there are souls to harvest. Use me! Amen.

"Revival Is Coming," *The Pentecostal Evangel.*

Week 28—Day 1
Repentance Unto Life

READ ACTS 11:18; 20:21; 26:20; ROMANS 10:10

In Acts 11:18, we read that God granted "repentance unto life" to those who sought His forgiveness, accepted Christ, and were converted. The Lord is not willing that any should perish.

The apostle Paul speaks of "repentance toward God, and faith toward our Lord Jesus Christ." Jesus said, "There is joy in the presence of the angels of God over one sinner that repenteth." He did not say that there is rejoicing over any sinner who merely believes in Christ without repenting and receiving Him. Many scriptures show us that repentance always precedes saving faith. Nothing is saving faith that does not believe "unto righteousness," for "with the heart man believeth unto righteousness." Even John Calvin wrote, "It is faith alone which justifies, and still the faith which justifies is not alone. Ears, feet, and hands are given to us at the same time that our eyes are, yet it is the office of the eye alone to see." In like manner, repentance, love, obedience are the veritable companions of faith.

—*Mrs. F. F. Bosworth*
n.d.

Father, please help me to understand and embrace true repentance so that, should it ever be necessary to repent once more of any fresh infraction, I'll be quick to do it. In Jesus' name. Amen.

From a tract titled, *The "Why?" and "How?" of Salvation.*

Day 2

Confession Essential to Forgiveness

READ PSALM 51; MATTHEW 21:28–29

Return to God and confess when you have been wrong. Go before the Lord and lay open the depth of your guilt. Tell Him you deserve the punishment of sin, but that you come for mercy through the merits of His Son and your Substitute. Come with only one plea: "Thy blood was shed for me!"

In accordance with your confession, the Lord says, "If their . . . hearts be humbled, and they then accept of the punishment of their iniquity: then will I remember My covenant" (Lev. 26:41). Then God can forgive. But so long as you controvert this point, and will not admit that God is right, or admit that you are wrong, He cannot forgive.

When coming back to God for pardon, come with all you have. Lay it at His feet. Come with your body to offer as a living sacrifice upon His altar. Come with your soul and all its powers, and yield them in willing consecration to your God and Savior. Come with your spirit and yield it to His Spirit.

—*Mrs. F. F. Bosworth*
n.d.

Lord, I come to You with the truth as my confession. Forgive me, as necessary, and restore me to close fellowship with You. In Jesus' name. Amen.

From a tract titled, *The "Why?" and "How?" of Salvation.*

Day 3
Once and for All

READ MARK 8:34–38

I made my decision once and for all. I said, "Yes, Lord—I will be Your servant! I will follow You, together with my husband. I want to go all the way. I want Your anointing. I want Your power to work through me. I want to study Your Word. I want to be Your representative and messenger, and to teach and proclaim Your Word everywhere!"

Within a few weeks our beautiful furniture was sold; everything we had, except a few suitcases of clothing, was disposed of. We started out in faith, like Abraham and Sarah, not knowing where God would lead. But we were full of joy, confident that the Lord was with us.

For over five years we never had a bed to call our own. Our babies knew nothing of the freedom that most children enjoy—no fine toys, no nice yards, almost nothing to call their own. Different beds, changing climates, strange food, but they were healthy, happy, and contented, and blessed in so many ways. From then until now, my husband and I have walked together, prayed and fasted together, taught and preached together . . . I would not trade those suitcases today for the loveliest house in the world!

—*Daisy Washburn Osborn*
1990

Lord, I make my decision once and for all; use me, no matter the cost. In Jesus' name, Amen!

The Woman Believer (Tulsa, OK: OSFO Publishers, 1990).

Day 4

Prayer and Faith

READ MATTHEW 19:23–26

So silent, yet irresistible,
Thy God shall do the things impossible.
Oh, question not henceforth what thou canst do;
Thou canst do nought. But He will carry through
The work where human energy has failed,
Where all thy best endeavors had availed
Thee nothing. Then, my soul, wait and be still;
Thy God shall work for thee His perfect will.
If thou wilt take no less, His best shall be
Thy portion now and through eternity.

—*Freda Hanbury*
December 1919

Lord, fulfill Your work, Your perfect work, in me. In Jesus' name. Amen.

The Pentecostal Evangel.

Day 5
A Root of Bitterness

READ EPHESIANS 4:31–32; HEBREWS 12:14–15

We have found that a great difficulty in the way of divine healing is the lack of divine love flowing in the hearts of God's children. It is remarkable how many times we have found some child of God cherishing a secret grudge against another Christian. Sometimes it has been a thing which has long been buried and almost forgotten. The sting of it may even be past, but it has been a "root of bitterness."

In Hebrews 12:14–15, we see there is a diligent looking unto Jesus, that such a root of bitterness might not spring up, and if it does spring up in our hearts, it is because we have failed of the grace of God which would have kept us from any such sorrow or misery. No matter how far in the past such a thing has been, it must be confessed, put under the blood, and—if possible—confession must be made to the one against whom there has been ill feeling.

It is not a question of our being right or wrong; we may have been right in the first place, but our lack of love for our neighbor made us wrong in God's sight.

—*Carrie Judd Montgomery*
December 1919

Lord, root out any bitterness in me and help me to deal with it as Your Word directs. In Jesus' name, please fill me with love for my neighbors. Amen.

"Some of the Hindrances to Healing," *The Pentecostal Evangel.*

Weekend
The Debt of Love

READ ROMANS 13:8–14

Dear one, if you will honestly yield your whole heart to the Lord for Him to search through and through, He will do so tenderly and faithfully, and will show you if there is lurking in its hidden depths a root of bitterness that is keeping back His healing life.

We must have an active love in our hearts for all of God's children, and also for all our enemies. "Love is the fulfilling of the law." We owe to everyone the debt of love, and as we yield to the Holy Ghost, who sheds abroad in our hearts the love of Christ, He will enable us to pay it.

—*Carrie Judd Montgomery*
December 1919

Lord, search me for any part of me that does not love others, and empower me to do it by Your Spirit. In Jesus' name. Amen.

"Some of the Hindrances to Healing," *The Pentecostal Evangel.*

Week 29—Day 1

God's Warning to Murmurers

READ DEUTERONOMY 28:47–48; ROMANS 1:21

A murmuring spirit is often the cause of lack of victory. When the children of Israel murmured, they grieved and angered God. We are commanded to "offer the sacrifice of praise to God continually"—not merely with our hearts but with our lips. And if we obey this command there will not be much room left for murmuring.

Among the terrible sins spoken of in Romans chapter 1, we read, "Neither were they thankful." In fact, it would seem that many awful sins followed because the people were not thankful. May the Lord enable us to "give Him thanks always, for all things," even as He has commanded.

—*Carrie Judd Montgomery*
December 1919

Father, please forgive me for murmuring, complaining, and for not being thankful in all things. I choose to praise You and give thanks with both my heart and my lips. Help me to do this continually. In Jesus' name. Amen.

"Some of the Hindrances to Healing," *The Pentecostal Evangel*.

Day 2

Press Through!

READ MATTHEW 11:12; LUKE 8:43–48

The Bible records, "The kingdom of God suffereth violence, and the violent take it by force." This is pleasing to the Lord, who wants us to press through all opposing forces of the enemy, and to receive from Him all that He has bought for us by His precious blood.

We see that Jesus was pleased with the Syrophoencian woman who would not be denied, even when He answered her not a word, and afterward, when He seemed unwilling to grant her petition. When talking to her, He called healing "the children's bread." And praise God—that's what it is! But the woman answered well, persisted, and received. She pressed through.

He was also pleased with the woman who had the issue of blood, who pressed her way through all the crowd to touch the hem of His garment.

—*Carrie Judd Montgomery*
December 1919

> *Lord, I press through to You, against the obstacles of the enemy. Thank You for the victory that You purchased by Your blood for me! Amen.*

"Some of the Hindrances to Healing," *The Pentecostal Evangel.*

Day 3
Learn God!

READ 2 CORINTHIANS 3:17–18; TITUS 1:15–16

There are a thousand things you don't have to know to get to God, but you have to get to God! We are here to learn God, not just about Him. We can know a thousand things about Him, and be able to answer all of the things about Him, and not really know God!

A lot of people think you've got to do something religious to know Him; nothing doing! The Bible says we are changed simply by beholding Him.

I want you to know God. We are going to spend our whole future with Him: Isn't that wonderful? So we need to know Him, give Him glory, spend time in His presence, learn Him. This is why Jesus said, "Take my yoke upon you, and learn of Me." Learn who He is, what He wants, how He moves, what God responds to. After all, we are not responsible to anybody but Him. And then when we walk before God and do His will, we may meet some opposition from time to time from carnality, but the end will vindicate you! Learn God!

—*Hattie Hammond*
n.d.

Lord, I want to know You—not simply about You.
Help me to learn You, as I seek You in prayer and in
the Word. In Jesus' name. Amen.

Audiocassette titled, "How to Pray," from a chapel service at Christ for the Nations.

Day 4
Go In and Shut the Door

READ PSALM 19:12–14; JOHN 20:19

Go into thy closet, He says, and shut the door! Oh, what a secret! Shut everything out! Get rid of "Old Man Reason." Everyone of us has a lawyer inside of us who wants to constantly reason with God. Our mind starts operating and going around and around like a stuck record. We have to shut that out. Shut the door!

Shut the door against your own body. Get down on your knees, and if you are there very long, your knees will begin to cry out, "I'm tired! Get me up from here!" Shut that out. Speak to your tired bones and say, "Be quiet—I'm going to pray!" Your stomach will cry out, "I'm hungry!" No! Shut the door! Stay before God, praying behind closed doors. And your Father, who hears in secret, will reward you openly.

—*Hattie Hammond*
n.d.

Lord, help me to go into my prayer closet and shut the door, shut everything out except You. Develop the discipline of prayer within me. In Jesus' name. Amen.

Audiocassette titled, "How to Pray," from a chapel service at Christ for the Nations.

Day 5
Women Who Partner With God

READ JOHN 5:20; 14:12–14

God wills material blessings for women, but they must apply themselves in creative thinking, in enterprise, and in industry, in a competitive world as the Proverbs 31 woman did—and as all successful people must do.

Allow your indigenous talents and innate abilities to come to life: not at the expense of your family and marriage, but because of them. Become alert to your own potential. Reach out and become a learner. Upgrade your own attitude. Decide that God is depending on you as a woman to accomplish His work as much as He depends on any man. Believe for Him to impart His wisdom to you. There is nothing impossible for God and the woman believer.

—*Daisy Washburn Osborn*
1990

Lord, bring forth my creativity and potential and empower me by the Holy Spirit to use these innate gifts and talents to the fullest, to glorify You. In Jesus' name. Amen.

The Woman Believer (Tulsa, OK: OSFO Publishers, 1990).

Weekend

What Is Your Financial Role?

READ HOSEA 10:12; MATTHEW 13

As a woman believer, is your attitude, "My place, as a woman, is to concede to life and to fulfill whatever role others expect of me"? Or is it, "As a woman, I choose to identify with God in His love plan for people. I understand that money can be a sacred tool for soulwinning. I will be God's partner to reach hurting human persons and to bless them as the Proverbs 31 woman did—starting with my own family."

Giving to reach souls is a ministry in itself. When the woman believer invests her money to reach the unsaved, she is as much a minister or a missionary as the one who goes and announces the Good News.

—*Daisy Washburn Osborn*
n.d.

Lord, I partner with You financially; teach me to sow my financial seed where it will best accomplish a good crop for You. In Jesus' name. Amen.

The Woman Believer (Tulsa, OK: OSFO Publishers, 1990).

Week 30—Day 1

If You Ever See Jesus . . .

READ LUKE 19:2–9; HEBREWS 2:9–10

In 1946 two missionaries returned, defeated and heart-broken, from the mission field of India. By the following year they had settled in a pastorate position in Oregon, but this young married couple had felt a stirring. Upon hearing of the death of Charles Prince, the pastor went to the altar and began to weep aloud. He could not contain his grief as he thought of the great pioneers of the faith who had recently died—Smith Wigglesworth, Aimee Semple McPherson, Gipsy Smith, Myer Pearlman. Where would the suffering and sick go for help?

A short time later the answer came: The young minister heard a lady preach a wonderful message, entitled, "Seeing Jesus." This woman, who had taken over Charles Price's itinerary, exhorted, "If you ever see Jesus, you'll never be the same." The next morning he was awakened by a vision. Jesus walked into the room. No words could tell what he saw that day, but seeing Jesus changed his life.

Soon after they went back out into the world and preached to millions, confirming the gospel with signs and wonders. That young couple was T. L. and Daisy Osborn—changed by the preaching of a woman!

—*Hattie Hammond*
n.d.

Father, thank You that You have used women throughout history to change lives. Amen.

Taken from a historical devotional.

Day 2
The Greatest Battle

READ ROMANS 7:23–25; 8

Sometimes you have the greatest battle with the enemy when you get on your knees and mean real business with God. Some mornings I have gone into my room and waited, and as I have tried to get my mind on God, it seemed as though it went around like a phonograph record. I thought of everything and everybody in the world.

That's all right; God is dealing with you, trying to draw you to Himself. The old flesh is kicking and pulling and drawing from the other side. But God is pulling too, so wait. Just be quiet. He is there; He is waiting. He sees you on your knees, but He wants to know whether you mean business. And when you prove you mean business, and stay there, lay hold of God. You are sure to get something from Him. The world is looking for reality. The world wants to see reality in the lives of professing men and women. They are standing at our church doors and crying through our windows. Shall we not be still before God until our souls are filled and flooded and saturated again with God? Then we shall see revival.

—Hattie Hammond
August 1928

Lord, I am determined to wait on You; help me to quiet my soul so that I think of nothing but You! In Jesus' name. Amen.

"Drawing Nigh to God," *The Pentecostal Evangel.*

Day 3

A Secret Source of Strength

READ PSALM 81

There is a secret source of strength for this battle we are engaged in, which we will be wise to avail ourselves of constantly. It is in communing with Jesus.

Holding a feast with Him in our hearts, worshiping Him, loving Him, adoring Him, conscious of His presence continually—here is the instrument perfectly adjusted to the Master's touch. The emptied vessel is filled with the constantly inflowing and outflowing water of life. His breath is our breath. The life that flows in the Head of the body is the life that flows in the veins of the body, and this walk of communion is a conscious reality to us. Our eyes are not on the waves at our feet, but they rest on the face of Jesus.

Distractions and distresses come in only when our gaze falls. When we look down at the sea of life over which we are walking, restless, unstable, changing, that restlessness seizes us. We are perplexed and beaten about by waves. We are sinking out of our element. We do not belong in that sea. Those waves should concern us little. Our walk is above them.

—*Zelma E. Argue*
October 1921

Lord, I want to commune with You so closely that I am always conscious of Your precious presence. Lead me there, Lord. In Jesus' name. Amen.

"Communion With Jesus," *The Pentecostal Evangel.*

Day 4

Limits for Women?

READ 2 TIMOTHY 4:1–5

Christian women in the church are expected to be saved, Spirit-filled, and gifted by God. Yet their ministry is tightly circumscribed and arbitrarily limited to submissive and subservient roles. Therefore, their potential and their creative talents for ministry and leadership are rarely included in the community of believers.

Every Christian woman has a noble and worthy reason to succeed in life. That reason is to be a partner and a co-worker with God in communicating the Good News to hurting and needy people. "Preach to every creature" is another way of saying "communicate the Good News to people." Develop the means and the methods of reaching out to your world in effective ministry.

—*Daisy Washburn Osborn*
1991

Lord, I trust You to help me soar above the limits and fulfill my divine destiny in Christ. In Jesus' name. Amen.

New Life for Women (Tulsa, OK: OSFO Publishers, 1991).

Day 5

Fervent Prayer

READ JAMES 5:16

James says the "effectual, fervent prayer of a righteous man availeth much." It is one thing to say a prayer, and quite another to pray a prayer—to prevail in prayer with God. Prevailing prayer leads us to a nearness with God. We get intimate and stand in holy awe before God. Prevailing prayer conquered Esau, and stopped the mouths of the lions when Daniel was in the lions' den. Elijah prevailed with God, and it rained not for three and a half years. Again, he prayed, and there was great rain. Esther prayed the prayer of faith for her people, the Jews, and they were delivered from Haman.

The prayer of faith and fastings bring the power of God. Bloody Mary (Mary Queen of Scots) said, "I fear the prayers of John Knox more than all the armies of Europe." Her death warrant was signed in heaven as John Knox cried, "Give me Scotland or I die!" Martin Luther also prevailed with God when the emperor of Germany resolved to proclaim religious tolerance. Luther exclaimed, "Deliverance has come, deliverance has come." When the church of Christ as a body gets down to this kind of prayer, we will see the gifts brought back more fully, and see the world brought to Christ.

—*Mrs. Ida McCoy*
n.d.

Lord, I purpose to prevail in prayer with You. Teach me how to do it by Your Spirit. Amen.

Neglected Themes and Helpful Hints (n.p., n.d.).

Weekend

The Valley of Baca

READ PSALM 84:6

The enemy will try to get you to worry. He will tell you there is no use to try—that you will have to wait until the skies clear a little . . . 'til things do not look so somber. But that is a lie, dearly beloved. The Lord just wants to pass you through your Valley of Baca weeping), and make it a well springing up unto everlasting life. He will make you an overcomer.

He will give you the overcomer's reward. The valley of depression is a very poor place to buy oil for your lamps if they are going out, for the kind sold there is mostly tears, and tears will not burn. He is sending you out today to love and cheer sinners by telling them of Him. He has given you a talent. Let it work. He has put you here for a purpose—to shine forth His love, peace, joy, longsuffering, meekness, and quietness of spirit. How are you going to do it if you let the devil keep you worried? So long as you keep worrying, you are minding the things of the flesh.

—*Mrs. G. F. Engblom*
November 1925

Lord, make me an overcomer so that when the enemy comes, I can resist his efforts to make me worry and become depressed. Encourage me by Your Spirit, and in Your Word. Amen.

"The Place of Worry in the Christian Life," *The Pentecostal Evangel.*

Week 31—Day 1
The Patience of Job

READ JOB 42:10–17

The patience, trust, and faith of Job will always be a memorial to Christian hearts. Try as he would, Satan could not cause Job to waiver one iota. What an example to God's children today! H. G. Spafford must have thought of Job when he wrote:

> Though Satan should buffet,
> Tho' trials should come,
> Let this blest assurance control,
> That Christ has regarded my helpless estate,
> And hath shed His own blood for my soul.

Though the tempests rage around us and the waters of sorrow flood over our souls, and by grief our hearts are broken, Christ is abundantly able to keep that which we have committed unto Him. The Lord allows Satan to tempt us to the breaking point, but He will not permit him to conquer our souls if our hearts are stayed on Him.

—*Miss Marjorie Price*
March 1932

Father, thank You that You give me that same patience, trust, and faith as Job. Empower me to stand fast, as did Job. In Jesus' name. Amen.

Golden Grain.

Day 2
The Things That Last

READ JOHN 4:34–36

Catherine Booth was marked by lifelong passion for souls. In early girlhood engaged to marry a socially prominent man, she saw their interests growing further apart so, much to her mother's disapproval, she decided she must break the engagement. Some years later, marrying William Booth, she launched at once into earnest soulwinning efforts.

Her attempts at first were not made in public, and were in a small way. One Sabbath evening, on her way to service, the thought occurred to her, *By turning into some of these houses, speaking to and inviting these careless sinners, would you not be doing God more service, and acting more like your Redeemer, than by going to God's house yourself?*

Trembling, with a sense of guilt, she looked up to heaven and said, "Lord, if Thou wilt help me, I will try." Suffering an agony of timidity at first, she spoke to a group of women sitting on a doorstep. As they listened, she was encouraged, so she passed on to the next group; thus, moving on down the street, knocking at closed doors, praying whenever possible, urging all to salvation.

—*Zelma Argue*
1935

Lord, give me that kind of passion for soulwinning! In Jesus' name. Amen.

Garments of Strength (Springfield, MO: Gospel Publishing House, 1935).

Day 3
Heartfelt Intercession

READ EZEKIEL 3:17–20

Catherine of Sienna, back in the Middle Ages, so interceded for souls, weeping at the altar of prayer, and crying, "Lord, promise me that You will save them," that she suffered bodily anguish.

—*Zelma Argue*
1935

Lord, I have merely scratched the surface of touching Your heart for the lost. Please fill me with a passionate desire to see the lost accept Christ, and empower me to boldly share the gospel with those around me. Fill me with the fervent desire to pray for souls. In Jesus' name. Amen.

Garments of Strength (Springfield, MO: Gospel Publishing House, 1935).

Day 4

Not Ready to Launch Out?

READ LUKE 5:3–6

Do you feel that you are not ready to launch out? My counsel is, "Just begin." You are ready for your first step now. You will become ready for tomorrow's challenges by the steps you take today.

- You will learn by teaching.
- You will gain by giving.
- You will reap by sowing.
- You will grow by sharing.

This is God's formula for your success and fulfillment. By choosing to be a part of God's plan for people, you are ultimately fulfilling God's dream for you.

—*Daisy Washburn Osborn*
1990

Lord, help me to just launch out and do it—get involved in soulwinning and ministry, whether or not I feel that I am ready. Give me boldness and guide and empower me by Your Spirit. In Jesus' name. Amen.

The Woman Believer (Tulsa, OK: OSFO Publishers, 1990).

Day 5

The Answer Is on the Way

READ LUKE 22:39–46

One afternoon I felt a heavy burden to pray. I began to travail greatly in the Spirit, and it did not lift. The next week I stayed before the Lord and a great deal of the time prayed with such fervency that I knew I was touching God. Many times I would groan in the Spirit, and others would lay hands on me, but I had no relief. All I could do was pray.

It seemed the eyes of the Lord were looking right through me. I knew I must seek Him until I found relief. Then, after this had lasted for a week, I asked my husband to pray for me, and peace came into my spirit. Then in a vision I saw Jesus in the distance, kneeling. I could clearly see His soft brown hair as he knelt beside a rock— resembling a picture I had seen of Him kneeling in Gethsemane. I began to rejoice in the Spirit, as the Lord said to me, "All week you have been in Gethsemane." I knew then that the answer was on the way.

The following Sunday the power of God began to fall, souls were saved and filled, and bodies healed. It all began through intercessory prayer.

—*Carmen Thacker Goodwin*
1992

Lord, lead me into travail for souls. Use me to help pray in a mighty outpouring of Your Spirit. In Jesus' name. Amen.

Springtime and Harvest (Self-published, 1992).

Weekend

The Net of Unbelief

READ MATTHEW 17:14–21

One Sunday morning God had whispered to my heart and given me a revelation to deliver to the people. It seemed there was a long table, and at one end the apostles and prophets were seated, eating and drinking, enjoying the good things of God. It seemed there was every good thing to eat imaginable at that table. At the other end were people of the Pentecostal movement who were just looking at the things on the table before them.

Between them and the food, there was a net, across which was written the word, "unbelief." These people were satisfied to look at the food, and enjoyed watching others make use of it. Nevertheless, no one lifted a hand to lift the net and reach for the food so that they might too enjoy the power and the presence of the Lord, as did the apostles and the prophets gathered at the opposite end.

—*Hattie Hammond*
n.d.

Lord, deliver me from unbelief. Increase my faith. In Jesus' name. Amen.

Taken from the diary of Hattie Hammond.

Week 32—Day 1
Reject the Negatives

READ MARK 14:1–9

You may have been verbally or physically abused as a child. You may have been told that you are worthless and that you could never amount to anything. Never believe any person or group or system that negates your individual person. They are not true. Reject their influences. Refuse their doctrines. Shut out their voices. Reject their dogmas, their scrutiny, their assessments.

The only influence that can ever really put you down is your own attitude. It can only happen to you through your own choice to listen and to give credit to someone who demoralizes you. Turn them off. Shut them out, and walk into your wonderful, positive world.

You are created in God's image; you have tremendous value. He paid a big price for you. He determined your worth by giving His best, His only Son, to redeem you and restore you to Himself as His friend and partner. Does that tell you anything about your value?

—*Daisy Washburn Osborn*
1986

Father, thank You for redeeming me from the effects of verbal and physical abuse. I choose to no longer listen to those voices from the past—voices that demoralized me and cut me to the core. I forgive those who abused me; now help me to forget. In Jesus' name. Amen.

5 *Choices for Women Who Win* (Tulsa, OK: OSFO Publishers, 1986).

Day 2
The Fertile Valley

READ PSALM 23

In following the Lord in obedience, David had been descending into the valley with the Lord. The valley looked so dark and formidable, but David found that with Jesus, the valley of tears was a well of living water. And the waters that we pass through are only pools filled with the rains from heaven, for Jesus is leading us.

My friend, the fertile land is not upon the mountaintop, but down in the valley! The valley is the place from which one emerges with spiritual strength. No wonder the Bible says, "In everything give thanks, for this is the will of God in Christ Jesus concerning you." And so David, mounting the hilltops and passing through the valleys of life, following the Lord, finally caught a glimpse of the end of his journey of eternity beyond. He wrote, "Surely goodness and mercy shall follow me all the days of my life, and I shall dwell in the house of the Lord forever."

You need not go through life alone. Jesus wants to lead you through. He will brighten your way.

—*Rev. Edna Jean Horn*
n.d.

Lord, take my hand and lead me through the valley.
Help me to learn what it is that You are trying to teach
me, and make me strong. Amen.

Condensed from a radio sermon titled, "Through the Valley With God."

Day 3
While There Is Yet Time

READ HEBREWS 3:12–19

There is a famous story of Queen Elizabeth I of England who, as she lay dying, pleaded for more time, offering her royal wealth for just a little more time. Oh, how trifling things deceive us with their insistent demands for our attention. How they would steal our opportunities to spend our time for the things that count for time and eternity!

The wise man or woman is on guard to weight the golden hours down with every possible jewel for eternity. The opportunity is with us. We may take it or lose it. Often the Spirit of God whispers to us, if we are attentive enough to listen, and He warns us to act for God at the moment when it will most count. Let us act while there is yet time.

—*Zelma Argue*
1935

Lord, please deliver me from giving attention to life's distractions. Help me instead to listen to the Spirit's leadings to take advantage of every opportunity to lay up eternal treasure in Your kingdom. In Jesus' name. Amen.

Garments of Strength (Springfield, MO: Gospel Publishing House, 1935).

Day 4
The Praise Cure

READ PSALM 100:4; 103:1–17

The Bible says, "Enter into His gates with thanksgiving, and into His courts with praise." We can stand on God's Word for salvation and healing after we have met God's conditions and have grounded every weapon of rebellion, and can praise our way through to perfect, manifested victory.

This, I call the "praise cure." It never fails when the praise is the outflow of a heart resting on God's unchanging Word.

—*Dr. Lillian B. Yeomans*
March 1924

> *Lord, I choose to praise You for Your glorious works—through history, and in my life and in the lives of my loved ones. Thank You, Lord, for salvation and healing and for the Holy Spirit. In Jesus' name. Amen.*

The Pentecostal Evangel.

Day 5
No Resistance

READ PHILIPPIANS 2:5–13

When you get near the lovely Christ, look at Him. Just look at Him. There's no struggle of any kind, no war raging in Him. He's not battling on the inside within Himself—not like us, when we want to do good but evil is present to resist us. None of that is within Him. None of that indecision. No rebellion.

He says, "I do the things which please my heavenly Father. I just delight in it." There is no resistance in Him—no resistance whatsoever. There is no resistance to the will of God. He surrendered unto death. He knew what God's plan was for Him, so He surrendered to it. We need to say that too: "I'll go that way, Father. I'll walk with You, even if it means death on the cross."

—Hattie Hammond
n.d.

Lord, I'll go Your way, even if it means death on Your cross. Take the resistance from my Spirit. In Jesus' name. Amen.

Audiocassette titled "Life Bearers," from a chapel service at Christ for the Nations.

Weekend

Never Be Afraid to Wait

READ PSALM 27:14; 37:7; 62:5–8

Never be afraid to wait quietly before God. Never be afraid to wait on the Lord. We can well afford to wait on Him. Isn't it beautiful when He stills this human thing, and He gets through to us? He has to quiet the human thing in us that is just racing and ranting all the time. That's one of the reasons why so many of our prayers aren't answered, and we don't get from God what we would like to have.

I was glad to tell a man in Kansas once, who wanted the baptism in the Holy Spirit but who would pray for five minutes like a house afire and then be up and gone. "Brother, you don't stay long enough for Him to do anything! Just pray Amen, and you're gone!" And then the angels come, and then Jesus comes, and then the Father comes—and they say, "Where is that man who asked for the baptism in the Holy Ghost? He's gone!" So that man got down at the altar, and before that meeting was over, He had the baptism of the Holy Spirit.

—*Hattie Hammond*
n.d.

Lord, teach me to wait on You so that You can do the work of the Holy Spirit within me. Forgive me for my quick prayers and forgetting to wait on Your reply. In Jesus' name. Amen.

Audiocassette titled, "How to Pray," from a chapel service at Christ for the Nations.

Week 33—Day 1
Watch Yourself Grow

READ PHILIPPIANS 3:8–14

Any woman who sees her identity in Jesus Christ is one who has discovered her personal choice of power in life. She is a peacemaker. She is humble. She is willing to serve any one, any time, any where. That kind of service is the greatest kind of leadership, and it is the only true road to real happiness and achievement.

Look at what you have, at what you know, at what you can do. Do not look at what you do not have, or what you do not know, or what you cannot do. Do what you can do. Give what you can give. Be what you are. Share what you know. And watch yourself grow.

Jesus said, in essence, that "to be the greatest in My kingdom, to be a believer, a follower of Me, a disciple, and a graduate with My highest degree of honor is to be a servant to all."

—*Daisy Washburn Osborn*
1990

Father, thank You for giving me a servant's heart. I serve You and others willingly. In Jesus' name. Amen.

The Woman Believer (Tulsa, OK: OSFO Publishers, 1990).

Day 2
He Is Our Reward

READ MATTHEW 6:33; HEBREWS 11:6

The Holy Spirit is only the potential for power. It is our ministry that urges us manward with an effectiveness and power that we so desperately need today. But I believe it is ridiculous for us to think that we can effectively minister to men without first learning how to minister to God. As we minister to the Lord and soak ourselves in Him, we come to the place where He is our reward. Not ministry, not things, not healings, not financial prosperity—but the Lord Himself is our reward! He is our life, our everything.

So many people use their religion as a coin to purchase the benefits of God. Lord, forgive us! They use their ministries to glorify themselves and their energies to do the work of the Lord. How horrible! If we would only do what God commanded—seek first His kingdom—everything else would fall into place. And He would get the glory. We would even find that God speaks, answers prayers, and blesses us with His presence much more powerfully when we minister to Him instead of merely petition Him.

—*Roxanne Brandt*
1973

Lord, teach me to minister to You in such a devoted way that I know unequivocally that You are my reward. In Jesus' name. Amen.

Ministering to the Lord (Springdale, PA: Whitaker House, 1973).

Day 3
Satan's Territory

READ LUKE 10:19

As long as we are in Satan's territory—the world—he will try to attack us. For this reason, we should constantly ask God to cover us and surround us with the blood of Jesus. Then we must believe that Satan cannot harm us because of the blood. Jesus said, "I give you power . . . over all the power of the enemy." This is the power of the blood of Jesus Christ, and by faith in His blood, to which we testify. The blood and the Word are all-powerful, but it takes true faith to set this never-failing power to work.

Use the blood and the Word against the enemy whenever he attacks you in spirit, soul, or body, and know that these take all power from the enemy. Also know that the enemy cannot put anything on you or keep anything from you, because God, who cannot lie, says the blood and the Word overcome Satan every time.

—*Mrs. C. Nuzum*
1928

Lord, thank You for the power in the blood and in the Word. Thank You that You have given that power to me, at Calvary. In Jesus' name. Amen.

The Life of Faith (Springfield, MO: Gospel Publishing House, 1928).

Day 4

Winning Principles

READ JEREMIAH 29:11–14

Celebrate the most valuable guiding principles of winning:

1. *Practice* the art of doing for others what you want them to do for you.
2. *Recognize* and value the unique person that you are.
3. *Accept* responsibility for the fact that your life is—and will always be—what you make it through your innate powers of choice, decision, and action.
4. *Absorb* the principle that failure is never final, so if you don't succeed the first time, keep trying.
5. *Realize* that whatever is worth your doing is worth doing the very best you can.
6. *Understand* that true happiness is having hope, experiencing love, and doing things for the betterment of people.
7. *Grasp* the winning criterion that what you learn, discover, prove, and know becomes the only power that you yourself can utilize in this world.

—*Daisy Washburn Osborn*
1986

Lord, I choose to apply these principles of winning. Help me to become a winner by the power of Your Spirit. In Jesus' name. Amen.

5 Choices for Women Who Win (Tulsa, OK: OSFO Publishers, 1986).

Day 5
Do You Believe?

READ MARK 9:17–29

Do you believe? Then prove it! Oh, how you need reckless faith—a faith that will dare to do. You have been tossing to and fro for so long, you have almost despaired. Hope is all but dead. Lift your troubled eyes for Jesus is coming for you right in the midst of your storm. He is the miracle-working Christ. Jesus specializes in the impossible. Is your case hopeless? Hopeless or otherwise, it is never too simple or too difficult for the Master to deliver.

Triumphantly, He bore you through the storms of life, of death. Victoriously, He comes to your pain-racked vessel and says, "Come; walk out. Put your feet overboard. I am thy Master. Don't stop to reason; just obey Me. I am the Lord who healeth all thy diseases. Come! Don't wait! Come now!"

Don't look at the impossible. Don't think of the cutting pain. Forget the fever; lift your eyes to Jesus. By faith, step overboard. Just the touch of His hand will turn your storm to calm.

—*Mildred Wicks*
n.d.

Lord, I'm stepping overboard by faith and coming out to meet You on the water. Help me to keep my eyes on You, where the miracles are. Amen.

The Dawn of a Better Day (Tulsa, OK: Standard Printing Co., n.d.).

Weekend

Steadfastness vs. Stubbornness

READ 1 CORINTHIANS 15:51–58

Stubbornness is simply pig-headedness—the determination to go my own way. *Steadfastness* is my will willing to go God's way. Now, in order to get my will to will with God, I must know what God's will is. Some people seem to think it the most difficult thing in the world to know the will of God. When my children were young, I wanted them to know my will—what I wished for them. I did not make it a puzzle for them to find out. Nor did I make it the biggest difficulty of their lives, so that they had to wonder about it and talk about it with one another, and marvel at whatever it was that mother wanted.

I wanted them to know my will, and I took every care that they should know it. Does God want to make it a puzzle to His children to know His will? I believe God wants me to know His will every bit of the time, and I believe He will take the utmost pain to make me understand, however slow and stupid I may be, so long as I want to. The Lord wants me to know His will, and if I am steadfast in seeking it—I shall know it!

—*Lydia Walshaw*
January 1940

Lord, teach me to know Your will; reveal it by Your Word and by Your Spirit. In Jesus' name. Amen.

"A Steadfast Faith," *The Pentecostal Evangel.*

Week 34—Day 1

Life-Bearers

READ LUKE 1:26–38

Life-bearers—that is what we are called to be! Carriers and bearers of this marvelous life of Jesus Christ. This is what was asked of Mary, when Gabriel came to her and asked her if she would bring life into this world. Would she surrender herself to bring life to the world? You and I are asked the same question today: The Holy Spirit asks, "Will you bring life into this awful world?" He asks, "Will you give yourself to Me to be an instrument in My hands so that I can bring life through you into the world?"

Well, if we are going to be an instrument of His life, we must first have that life within us. Jesus says, "I am come that you might have life. Life! I want you to have life! I am come that you might have life, and have it more abundantly." What does that mean? It means that we will have enough life to demonstrate the fact that we have His life within. Jesus is life; His whole message is life or death. Eat this and you'll live . . . Eat that and you'll die. Jesus was God's instrument of life. If we have Him within, then we become His *life-bearers*.

—Hattie Hammond
n.d.

Thank You, Lord, for using me to carry the light of Christ to a dark world. In Jesus' name. Amen.

Audiocassette titled, "Life-Bearers," from a chapel service at Christ for the Nations.

Day 2
Deadly Unbelief

READ MARK 16:14–18

Unbelief is the most deadly virus that can poison a human soul. It is the monarch sin, the parent sin, the A-1 sin, the masterpiece of Satan. It robs. It blinds. It dooms. And the devil is trying to chloroform even the Lord's redeemed with this pestilent potion. It might shock us if we could know how much unbelief there is in Christian hearts. How many lands of promise we are prevented from entering because of our unbelief!

Many of us, instead of trusting God and going forward, are being driven back from the border of the promised land of blessing, excluded from the peace which might be ours, bereft of joy, shut out from fullness of power, deprived of usefulness, disarmed for conquest, robbed of physical healing! Because of our doubting we look upon situations as though they can never be remedied, problems as though they can never be solved, conditions as though they can never be changed, diseases as though they can never be healed. Imperative indeed is the need of bringing our unbelieving hearts before the Lord Jesus Christ, crying out, "Lord, I believe; help thou my unbelief!" Doubt is fatal. We cannot afford to waiver in faith.

—*Louise Nankivell*
1957

Lord, I believe; help my unbelief! In Jesus' name. Amen.

"A Destructive Triad," *The Voice of Healing.*

Day 3

Awful Anxiety

READ PHILIPPIANS 4:4–9

In these perilous days of atomic threat, war clouds, confusion, difficulty, uncertainty, and the like, anxiety is increasingly setting into the hearts of people everywhere—into Christian hearts as well. There seem to be so many excuses for worry: the past, the present, the future, failing health, business reverses, ruined plans, disappointments, and an endless variety of things. But it is wrong to worry. Worry is a sin—an insidious sin.

It grieves the Lord, reflects upon His sufficiency, suppresses spiritual life, and damages personal testimony. The futility of anxiety is evidenced by the question Jesus asked: "Which of you by taking thought can add one cubit to his stature?" What can worry do for you? Nothing! Jesus knew the folly of worry, and instructed us not to be anxious about what we would eat, wear, or even about the problems of another day. In the same breath, He gave the simple, sure cure for anxiety—prayer: "In everything by prayer and supplication let your requests be made known unto God."

—*Louise Nankivell*
1957

Lord, please forgive me for worrying. I make my requests and supplications known before Your throne. Here are my needs! Thank You that You care for me, and that You'll meet the needs I have today. In Jesus' name. Amen.

"A Destructive Triad," *The Voice of Healing.*

Day 4

Unfounded Fear

READ MATTHEW 10

In a rather unusual broadcast, I heard figures given out to the effect that five thousand known fears that plague the human race have been tabulated. One told about a fear of going near the edge of the water—for the possibility of falling in. Another had a fear of being struck by something toppling from a high building. Still another was possessed with a phobia that someone would break in at night.

We are told that fear constricts the blood vessels, produces a poison which affects the bloodstream, and has been known at times to turn hair gray overnight, to paralyze, or even to cause death. Fear can render ineffective the very best medicines which could ever be prescribed. I have talked with heart cases in healing lines where the victims could not lay aside their nitroglycerin tablets because of their bondage to fear. Diabetics for the same reason could not give up their insulin. Faith had become inoperative because those dear children were ensconced in the grip of fear.

Beloved believer, God wants us to put away fear. "Fear thou not, for I am with thee." That should be plenty good enough reason not to fear.

—*Louise Nankivell*
1957

Lord, take any fear I may have and replace it with faith in Your Word. In Jesus' name. Amen.

"A Destructive Triad," *The Voice of Healing.*

Day 5
Cleansed From Sin

READ 1 JOHN 1:5–10

Young converts are in danger of being discouraged because after conversion they see sin and failure in themselves more clearly than ever before. Also, they discern much to be sin which hitherto they had excused, and are prone to be downcast thinking themselves worse than ever, forgetting that to see and hate sin is a result of the presence and work of the Holy Spirit in their hearts. Mrs. Booth wrote thus to a young woman tempted to despair:

> I am sure the devil has laughed at you, not because he has got you to sin, but because he has got you to give up. This is always his way, to tempt us to sin, and then to turn to us and say, "Now you will never have the impudence to seek forgiveness!" Great as your sin is, to despair and refuse to ask God's forgiveness is greater, because He promises, if we confess and forsake, to forgive. . . .

—*Helen Ramsay*
August 1930

Lord, thank You that I may come to You again and again as necessary for forgiveness. Create in me a clean heart; cleanse me from all sin, and renew a right spirit within me. In Jesus' name. Amen.

"Cleansing From Sin," *The Pentecostal Evangel.*

Weekend

The Presence of Light

READ PSALM 27

Some years ago, a friend and I were passengers on a Far Eastern railway. We had bought some sweets with which we were much pleased, and were eating them with utmost relish. We had purchased them in semi-darkness, but presently—when we found ourselves again in the light— we discovered to our disgust that our sweets were absolutely filthy! We cast them away with loathing! The light had made all the difference.

—*Helen Ramsay*
August 1930

Father, put the light on anything that's filthy and that must be cast away. Purify my heart and life. In Jesus' name. Amen.

"Cleansing From Sin," *The Pentecostal Evangel.*

Week 35—Day 1

Return

READ ZEPHANIAH 3

"She drew not near"—content to walk afar, apart
From God—her God—whose love once moved her heart
To song and fullest praise for victories complete
For guidance, help, communion close and sweet.
Like dew of morn her God one time had been,
As to His presence oft she entered in.
"Not near her God?" What intervening sin could be—
What boastful strength—What other vision see
To end such union as she once had known
While heaven's light upon her pathway shown
That now she drew no longer near to Him,
Walking defeated in earth's shadows dim?
Breathing, "Return, from whereso'er thou art, return."
Failure will end thy self-sought liberty.
Draw nigh to Me, I will draw nigh to thee;
And once again thy way My radiance shall show;
A fairer beauty yet thy life may show—
Only draw near. Outstretched My arms to thee;
Return, return, My child, draw near to Me.

—*Alice Reynolds Flowers*
October 1933

*Lord, thank You, that Your arms are outstretched and
ready to take me back whenever I move too far away.
Keep me close, Lord. In Jesus' name. Amen.*

Golden Grain.

Day 2

One Day at a Time

READ LUKE 9:21–26

One of his scholars once asked Rabbi ben Jochai, "Why did not the Lord furnish enough manna for Israel for a year, all at one time?"

The great teacher said, "I will answer you with a parable. 'Once there was a king who had a son to whom he gave a yearly allowance. It soon happened that the day on which the allowance was due was the only day in the year when the father saw the son. So the king changed his plan and gave his son day by day that which sufficed for the day. Now the son visited the father every morning, realizing his continual need of his father's love, companionship, wisdom, and giving.'"

So God deals a daily supply that supplication, communion, thanksgiving may be daily.

—*Hannah Whitall Smith*
November 1948

Lord, thank You for meeting my needs daily. In Jesus' name. Amen.

"Daily Thanksgiving," *The Pentecostal Evangel.*

Day 3
At Thy Feet

READ LUKE 10:38–42

At Thy feet—because I need thee:
Strength of youth shall faint and fail.
But the soul that truly waiteth
On the Lord shall e'er prevail.
At Thy feet—weakness forgotten;
At Thy feet—my wants supplied,
In the fountain of Thy fullness
All my need is satisfied. . . .

At Thy feet—because those nail-prints
Must impel to service new;
Waiting on thee maketh steady
All Thy gracious will to do.
At Thy feet—self-love forgotten,
Not a price too dear to pay;
I may go with message ready
Thus received from day to day.

At Thy feet—because the nearest
Place that I can draw to Thee;
Heart that yearneth for Thy coming
Just Thy face would only see. . . .

—*Alice Reynolds Flowers*
October 1933

*Lord, I bow before You, laying my life at Your feet. Use
me, Lord, as You see fit. In Jesus' name. Amen.*

Golden Grain.

Day 4

"I Have Overcome ..."

READ JOSHUA 6; COLOSSIANS 2:15

Joshua did not say, "Shout, for the Lord will give you the city." He said, "Shout, for the Lord hath given" it to you. Neither does our Lord say, "Be of good cheer; I will overcome the world." He says, "I have overcome" it. There is a mighty difference between the two, as great a difference as there is between meeting an army in full battle array, and meeting one routed and demoralized by an acknowledged defeat.

It is well known that as long as an army can keep the fact of its being conquered a secret from its conquerors, it can still make some show of resistance; but the moment it becomes conscious that its defeat is known, it loses all heart, becomes utterly demoralized, and has no resort left but to flee. The secret then lies in this: Meet our enemy as an already conquered foe, and not as one who has yet to be conquered.

—*Hannah Whitall Smith*
November 1948

Lord, I thank You that You have already overcome the enemy—and that because You have defeated the enemy, I have also. In Jesus' name. Amen.

"The Shout of Victory," *The Pentecostal Evangel.*

Day 5

Shout the Victory!

READ EZRA 3:10–13

Our usual way of meeting temptation has been, perhaps, with a cry for help. We have said over and over, "O Lord, save me!" Let us meet it hereafter with a shout of victory instead.

Let us say by faith, "He does save me!" The walls may look immovable as ever; and even prudence may say, "It is not safe to shout until the victory is actually won." But the faith that can shout in the midst of the sorest stress of temptation, "Jesus, save me—He saves me now," such a faith will be sure to win a glorious and speedy victory.

—*Hannah Whitall Smith*
November 1948

Lord, thank You for the "victory shout" in the midst of temptation, because You have won the victory for me! In Jesus' name. Amen.

"The Shout of Victory," *The Pentecostal Evangel.*

Weekend

Try This!

READ PSALM 47

Dear Christian, try this: Go out to meet your enemy, singing a song of triumph as you go, and I can promise you, on the authority of God's own Word, that according to your faith, it shall be unto you.

—*Hannah Whitall Smith*
November 1948

> *Father, let that song of triumph rise up within me so that next time I need to face the enemy, I will do so boldly, singing songs of Your victory! In Jesus' name. Amen.*

"The Shout of Victory," *The Pentecostal Evangel.*

Week 36—Day 1
Complete Freedom

READ EPHESIANS 3:14–21

As a woman, do not accept the submissive, silent, inferior role that you have been assigned by religion and culture. When you accept Jesus as Lord, you have no other master. He desires to express His love and leadership through you. The woman believer who accepts cultural restrictions and religious restraints is limiting Jesus, who craves expression through her. Only she can limit Christ at work in and through her life.

It takes courage for a woman to be what God has created her to be. She can be a Jesus-woman if she does not fear what people say about her; if she accepts God's will and lets go of the sanctimonious patriarchal indoctrination she may have inherited. I have seen the twins which religion gives birth to—*culture* and *tradition*. Religious women often go through life doing what they are *expected to do* rather than what they *choose to do*. They live with obligations rather than options. They bow to *rules and requirements* instead of enjoying the pleasure of responding to and of cultivating *God's ability within them.* The Holy Spirit in a woman is not meant to be silent. Believe it, and live in complete freedom.

—*Daisy Washburn Osborn*
1991

Thank You, Lord, that by Your Spirit, I am empowered to live victoriously, ministering as an ambassador of Christ. In Jesus' name. Amen.

Women and Self-Esteem (Tulsa, OK: OSFO Publishers, 1991).

Day 2
"Give Me Your Heart!"

READ ROMANS 10:6–10

You won't get anywhere as long as you keep your heart to yourself and just give God your activities, works, and service. That was Israel's sin. They wanted God's miracles and power, and everything else He could do for them, but they had no heart for God. That's the reason they were always running off into idol worship and sinning all the time; God didn't have their hearts.

That is the reason He continually called to them: "Give me thine heart. I want your heart!" The heart is the very center of you. It is the choice part of you. Out of the heart are the issues of life. He wants your heart. Get into a real "heart relationship" with Him.

God has a plan for your life, and it is a marvelous plan. But you will never come into that plan until you give God your heart—all of your heart.

—*Hattie Hammond*
n.d.

Lord, I give You my heart—all of it! In Jesus' name. Amen.

Audiocassette titled, "Give Me Your Heart," from a chapel service at Christ for the Nations.

Day 3

The Desires of Thine Heart

READ MARK 11:24; PSALM 37:4

In Mark 11:24, we read: "What things soever ye desire, when ye pray, believe that ye receive them, and ye shall have them." This promise, made by our blessed Lord, is so boundless in its grace, so unlimited in its rich provision, that weak faith often staggers before it. We feel like saying, "Can it be possible that God means just what this verse says? I am only a frail human being. How can He trust me to have right desires, so that He can fulfill them all?"

These questionings have undoubtedly gone through all of our hearts at one time or another. Let us see from God's Word what conditions must first be fulfilled before we can realize our blessed privileges. In Psalm 37:4, we read, "Delight thyself also in the Lord; and he shall give thee the desires of thine heart." Here again is the promise that our heart's desires will be granted, but there is a condition: We must delight ourselves in the Lord. It is one thing to delight in His mercy and His gifts; it is entirely another thing to delight ourselves in the Lord Himself, in the possible absence of all His gifts. Delighting ourselves in the Lord alone, our hearts are purified and our desires are His own desires within us.

—*Carrie Judd Montgomery*
September 1943

Lord, I yield completely to You; Thy will be done! In Jesus' name. Amen.

Day 4
"Thy Will Be Done . . ."

READ MATTHEW 6:6–15; 1 JOHN 5:14–15

Have you been brought to a place of lowliness and submission, where "Thy will be done" seems the only desirable expression of prayer? Then press on to have that will made clear, that you may know what Christ is longing for, and His own longing shall take possession of your own heart. Then there will be new meaning to the words, "What things soever ye desire, when ye pray, believe that ye receive them, and ye shall have them."

Having no longer any doubt about the will of God in each matter of prayer, you will be able to press your claim boldly, and to "believe that you take" (literal translation) "whatsoever ye desire." The same thoughts are brought out in 1 John 5:14–15: "If we ask anything according to his will, he heareth us: And if we know that he hear us, whatsoever we ask, we know that we have the petitions that we desired of him."

—*Carrie Judd Montgomery*
September 1943

Lord, I thank You that You have revealed Your will to me as I have delighted myself in You, in prayer. Thank You that I have been given the faith to believe that I have the requests I have asked of You. In Jesus' name. Amen.

"The Desires of Thine Heart," *The Pentecostal Evangel.*

Day 5
Those That Fear Him

READ PSALM 145:19; 1 KINGS 10:13

God's order of prayer is this: First, be emptied of all our own desires. Then be filled with Christ's desires, thus being filled with boldness to claim the fulfillment of these Spirit-born desires. Then to "know that we have the petitions we desired" by an assurance of faith before we can see or feel the answer. This is solid ground in prayer.

In fact, there is joy and wonderful glory in a trial of faith when we have the perfect confidence that we are already more than conquerors, and we are able to smile at Satan's vain attempts to overthrow our faith. "He will fulfill the desire of them that fear Him" Ps. 145:19). As King Solomon gave the Queen of Sheba all her desires, whatever she asked "of his royal bounty" 1 Kings 10:13), so is our King greater than Solomon. His "royal bounty" shall far exceed what we ask or think.

—*Carrie Judd Montgomery*
September 1943

Lord, thank You that You have granted me "the desires of my heart." I thank You that I have them today, whether or not I can yet see and feel them, for I have them by faith in Your Word. In Jesus' name. Amen.

"The Desires of Thine Heart," *The Pentecostal Evangel.*

Weekend

Lay Aside the Flesh

READ HEBREWS 12:1–2

Friends, the more established you become in the Lord, and the closer you come to God, the more you will lay aside and the more you will crucify the flesh. If you want to be like Jesus, you must lay aside the weights and sins which so easily beset mankind.

Some people are slow, like the turtle, so that they never get into a revival. They never seem to get far with God. They need to wake up, get on fire, and move a little faster!

—*Juanita Coe*
n.d.

Father, I want to be like Jesus; I choose the crucified walk, in order to draw nearer to You. In Jesus' name, give me the grace I'll need continually. Amen.

My Personal Message to You (n.p., n.d.).

Week 37—Day 1
Empty of Self

READ JEREMIAH 11:1–5; EPHESIANS 1:1–12

The other day I was reading something Madam Guyon had written on the emptying of self. She took Mary, the mother of Jesus, as an example of being emptied of self—perhaps the only woman God found who was empty enough for the incarnation of the Son of God. Empty. Void. Nothingness. Madam Guyon said that if Mary hadn't been absolutely void of self, an empty space for God to fill, when the Holy Ghost spoke to her heart, she could not have said, "Yes."

If there had been a self-life there, she would have spoken out like you and I in ourselves and immediately thought, *What will this mean? What would people say? What will Joseph think?* But no—there was absolutely nothing of the self-life, and she from the depths of her heart could say, "Yes, Lord, be it unto me according to Thy Word." That is what it means to be empty of self. There will be no question in your heart of what anybody thinks, only what Jesus thinks. It will mean inquiring of Him and not of one another.

—*Mrs. Marie Brown*
April 1923

Lord, I desire to become emptied of self so that Your power can infill me and flow out to others. Empty me, Lord, then fill me with the Holy Spirit. In Jesus' name. Amen.

From *Word and Work.*

Day 2

Filled With His Presence

READ ROMANS 12:1–2

Oh, for the emptying of ourselves to such a depth that He could fill us with Himself. Paul tells us how this can be made possible: "Present your bodies a living sacrifice, holy, acceptable unto God, which is your reasonable service. And be not conformed to this world: but be transformed by the renewing of your mind, that ye may be able to prove what is that good, and acceptable, and perfect will of God." How often we have put ourselves on the altar, and why was it that the offering was not consumed and this natural flesh of ours put to crucifixion and extinction of the old self-life?

Because, when we put ourselves on the altar of God, that moment our whole heart was looking up to Jesus and He saw it and accepted that sacrifice, but when the fire began to burn, to consume that offering, the old self began to feel it, and was not willing to go through the crucifixion in that place, in that fire. Therefore, they abandoned their offering and because of the persecution of trials, of tests, took themselves off the altar. God is faithful. "He is like a refiner's fire." He stands to prove that offering.

—Mrs. Marie Brown
April 1923

Lord, it hurts to die to self; yet I will to do it. Give me the grace to stay there on the altar until Your refining fire does its perfect work. Amen.

From *Word and Work.*

Day 3
Pride

READ PROVERBS 11:2; 13:10; 29:23; 1 JOHN 2:16

I had been praying that the Lord would take pride out of my life . . .

I was invited, with a group of ministers and workers, to a home for dinner. While eating, I noticed a brother's table etiquette: It seemed to me that he was eating with everything but his fist! As I looked at my brother, inwardly I was scolding him: *Thank God I am not like that!* My shoulders straightened up as I prided myself on my good table manners.

Then the dessert was served. I was so busy watching that man that I didn't notice how close to the edge of the table my pie was. As I brought down my fork, I emptied my pie into my lap, and the plate spilled onto the floor. Of course, I was very embarrassed and humiliated. No one knew what was actually going on inside me, but God had struck a blow to my pride. How I praise Him for the faithful Holy Spirit!

—*Hattie Hammond*
February 1936

Lord, please take pride out of my life. In Jesus' name. Amen.

Taken from the personal diary of Hattie Hammond.

Day 4
You Can Change Your World

READ ACTS 17:1–8

Women, only you can change your world! Choose to do just that. You do not need anyone's permission; you have been given your orders by the highest authority—your Lord.

You have been commissioned by Jesus. Do not wait for a council of elders, a board of theologians, an order of priests, or a cardinal to tell you what you can do. You have your orders. (See Mark 16:15.) You know what you are authorized to do. Just go and do it! Go and share Christ with your hurting world.

—*Daisy Washburn Osborn*
n.d.

Lord, I thank You that You have commissioned me to change my world. Give me wisdom and guidance, and show me what needs to be changed first! I yield myself to You, and accept Your commission into service. In Jesus' name. Amen.

Women and Self-Esteem (Tulsa, OK: OSFO Publishers, 1991).

Day 5
A Great Hindrance

READ PROVERBS 15:25; 16:5; MALACHI 4:1; 1 PETER 5:5

One of the greatest hindrances to getting God's best is often some form of pride. The Bible says, "God resisteth the proud."

There are many forms of pride. Some people are proud of their dress and appearance, and others of their opinions. We must ask God to deliver us from every form of pride, and make us humble, for the very next words of this verse are, " . . . but giveth grace unto the humble." We may think there is no pride in us, but we do not know our own hearts. God says, "I, the Lord, search the heart and try the reins."

Ask Him to search you out with that wonderful light from heaven. Ask Him to search out everything that hinders your having the blessings promised in His Word.

—*Carrie Judd Montgomery*
September 1927

Lord, thank You that You search my heart with the searchlight of the Holy Spirit. Please find and remove all pride—all hindrances of any type—and fill me with more of Your Spirit. In Jesus' name. Amen.

"What Hinders Your Healing?" *The Pentecostal Evangel.*

Weekend

True Darkness

READ 1 JOHN 2:9–12; JUDE

Some people say they are in the light, and they really think they are. But God says they are in darkness. Why? Because they have not forgiven some child of God who has done them wrong. They are blind to their own condition because 1 John 2:11 tells us, "He that hateth his brother is in darkness, and walketh in darkness, and knoweth not whither he goeth, because that darkness hath blinded his eyes."

I often wonder why people cannot see what wonderful blessing God has for them in Christ; but here, we are given a reason—hatred is darkness, and "that darkness hath blinded his eyes." Oh, dear one, that darkness of hating one's brother keeps many of God's children out of much blessing for body as well as spirit.

I am sure none of us wants to be in darkness, but if we allow in our hearts a grudge or critical spirit against one of God's children, it will surely blind our eyes. No matter what others do or how they act, God wants to deliver us from all lack of love and compassion.

—*Carrie Judd Montgomery*
September 1927

> *Father, please remove all grudges, all unforgiveness, all hatred from me—even from the depths, where I am unaware of these things—and fill me with Your love for my brethren. In Jesus' name. Amen.*

"What Hinders Your Healing?" *The Pentecostal Evangel.*

Week 38—Day 1
Faith and Love

READ PROVERBS 8:17–21

God says, "Faith worketh by love." Do you want a mighty faith? It will come when you have a mighty love.

Let us all ask Him this: "Fill me with Your love." We want to have great faith in God, that He might be glorified. I know sometimes there are people around us who are not lovable, but rather are disagreeable and hard to get along with. Then it is so sweet to say, "Jesus, You gave Yourself for me; therefore, I can take Your heart toward that one. I do not know just how You feel toward that one, but I know I shall feel as You do now."

Then I find that I begin to make excuses for them, much as a mother makes excuses for her child. We must pray to be filled with Christ's love. Then the devil has no soil in which to sow his wickedness and disease. He cannot plant his seeds in the soil of perfect love, but if we have a feeling of criticism or a grudge, the devil will plant seed there and it will grow very fast. Let us all seek today to be filled with the love of Christ so that His light and love will permeate us—spirit, soul, and body.

—*Carrie Judd Montgomery*
September 1927

Lord, fill me with Your love and empower me by Your
Spirit so that I can love even the unlovely. In Jesus'
name. Amen.

"What Hinders Your Healing?" *The Pentecostal Evangel.*

Day 2

A Little Encouraging Word

READ DEUTERONOMY 3:28; 1 SAMUEL 30:6;
2 CHRONICLES 31:4

Do not lose the blessing that lies hidden in your trials.

—*Carrie Judd Montgomery*
September 1927

Lord, help me to see into this season I am in. Help me to yield to the trials rather than resisting them, so that I can receive the blessing You have planned for me on the other side of the trials. Give me insight and understanding into that which You are working within me, for I say "Amen" to Your perfect work and trust You that it is all for my good. In Jesus' name. Amen.

"What Hinders Your Healing?" *The Pentecostal Evangel.*

Day 3
"We Are Going to the Orient"

READ 1 PETER 3:12–17

I was coming downstairs in my home one day, dusting the banisters with something as mundane as a dustcloth in my hands, when I felt the presence of Jesus. I said, "Jesus, You are here. . . ."

"Yes," He said. "We are going to the Orient."

"We are?" I knew that I knew that I knew that I would be ministering in the Orient. Wasn't it sweet for the Lord to say we? He didn't say, "You are going," or, "I am sending you," but, "We are going to the Orient."

I didn't write one letter. I didn't push one door open. I didn't say one word to anybody, but when He and I were alone, we talked it over. I said, "Jesus, You will have to get me ready. You'll have to prepare me. I don't know anything about the Orient." In about two weeks I got a long-distance call from Japan. They asked me to come and conduct a retreat for missionaries. I said, "Oh, yes. Jesus has already told me about this, and He and I are coming."

What do you suppose that dear missionary said? He said, "I'm so glad Jesus is coming too!"

—Hattie Hammond
February 1936

Lord, please guide me that clearly and prepare me for the things ahead. Increase my trust in You to open doors. Keep me from getting ahead of You by pushing them open myself! Amen.

Audiocassette titled, "Agelessness," from a chapel service at Christ for the Nations.

Day 4
The Power of the Blood

READ LUKE 22:20; HEBREWS 8:8–13

God says His people are like sheep in the midst of wolves. So He has given us a wonderful weapon to use— the blood of Jesus. This is our weapon, our shield, our hiding place. So long as we are walking in obedience to Him, we have a right to that blood every moment. It is the blood of our covenant with Him.

When some tribes and people enter into a covenant they prick the arm, or some part of the body, and put some of the blood of those who make the agreement with them. This means, if necessary, every drop of their lifeblood would be poured out to keep that covenant or pledge. When Jesus says, "This cup is the new testament of My blood," He means that every promise of the Book, every part of the covenant that He made with us, will be kept—even at the cost of His own lifeblood. Can you doubt a promise sealed like that?

—*Mrs. C. Nuzum*
1956

Lord, thank You for the blood of Your covenant. Reveal to me its full power, as well as how to apply it to my life for full victory. In Jesus' name. Amen.

The Life of Faith, Revised Edition (Springfield, MO: Gospel Publishing House, 1928, 1956).

Day 5
Life in the Blood

READ 1 JOHN 1:9; JOHN 5:53–58

The blood of Jesus represents the life. The Word says, "The blood is the life." Conversely, blood poured out represents death. See Genesis 9:4.) His covenant is the blood covenant, and it is the blood of our everlasting covenant— for time and eternity.

The blood cleanses. The Word tells us that our sins are blotted out by the blood. "If we confess our sins He is faithful and just to forgive us our sins, and to cleanse us from all unrighteousness." It is blessed to know that all our past sins are gone—blotted out forever. But He goes further than that: He removes those evil desires, cravings, and characteristics produced by habitually yielding to the urgings of the selfish nature. When we finally consecrate our all to Him and have our wills firmly set to obey Him and to live our lives by the law of love—that is when He puts within us a heart of flesh and the mind of Christ Jesus.

When you see anything in you that produces transgression, remember that His blood will take that away.

—*Mrs. C. Nuzum*
1956

Lord, thank You that there is life in the blood, and that I can apply it again and again to take away those things that would otherwise bring death. Thank You for Calvary. In Jesus' name. Amen.

The Life of Faith, Revised Edition (Springfield, MO: Gospel Publishing House, 1928, 1956).

Weekend

"Reckon Yourselves Dead"

READ ROMANS 6:8–18

After you have applied the blood to your transgressions, then the Bible says, "Reckon yourselves dead." Count on it; that is really true. The bearing about in your body the death of the Lord Jesus makes that thing in you really dead and separated from you. He says we are redeemed, not with corruptible things such as silver and gold, but with the precious, incorruptible blood of Jesus.

How often we ask other Christians to pray for us; but oh, how much more precious it is to know that these three are interceding for us—Jesus on the throne; the Holy Ghost in you, His temple; and the blood.

—Mrs. C. Nuzum
1956

> *Father, please reveal to me the power of Your blood. Help me to die to—remain dead to—my transgressions through the application of Your blood. Thank You for shedding it to pay for my sins. In Jesus' name. Amen.*

The Life of Faith, Revised Edition (Springfield, MO: Gospel Publishing House, 1928, 1956).

Week 39—Day 1
"Well Done!"

READ 2 TIMOTHY 4:5–8

News has reached us that dear Sister Whittemore of New York City has finished her course and gone to be with the Lord. Our sister was the founder of the Door of Hope work. She stated to the editor of the *Evangel* when he met her a year ago at Glad Tidings Tabernacle, New York: "The Lord has let me live to see ninety-seven Doors of Hope opened before He takes me home." We believe that thousands of rescued souls will welcome her in the glory, and that from the lips of her Master she has received the words, "Well done, good and faithful servant, enter thou into the joy of thy Lord."

EDITOR'S NOTE: *And all this when women couldn't "do anything" for God!*

—*Item from* The Pentecostal Evangel
February 1931

Lord, thank You for the inspiring testimony of one woman's life, and how You used her to save thousands of lost souls. Reveal Your plan to use my life, as I submit to the leadings of Your Spirit. In Jesus' name. Amen.

Day 2

Fire and Rain in India

READ EXODUS 3

In Mukti, India, a consecrated native woman was praying with a company of Hindu girls. They had spent days and nights in prayer, when suddenly the Latter Rain was outpoured in their midst, just as the Former Rain was given on the Day of Pentecost. Visible fire is said to have been seen upon one of the girls' beds, and when another girl ran to bring water to extinguish the flame, it was discovered to have been a different sort of fire—the kind which Moses saw at Mount Horeb in the burning bush . . . the same sort of fire that sat upon the heads of the hundred and twenty in the upper room.

One dear Hindu girl, filled with the Spirit, began to speak in English, which she had never learned. The message spoken through her was, "Jesus is coming soon!" Throughout India the Spirit fell and thousands were filled with the Holy Spirit. Without having studied the Word of God on this subject, and having no knowledge of such a biblical experience, the people at the time of their infilling began to speak in other languages as the Spirit gave them utterance.

—*Mattie Crawford*
1926

Lord, fill me with the Holy Spirit so that Your rain waters my spirit and Your holy fire burns bright in me. In Jesus' name. Amen.

The Baptism of the Holy Spirit (Los Angeles, CA: Publication and Executive Office, 1926).

Day 3
The Sack of Flour

READ MATTHEW 6:33–34

"Just guess the weight and put your address and telephone number on the slip!" Those were the instructions at the store, if I were to win a huge sack of flour. We could surely use the flour, and I thought, *How wonderful it would be if I won!*

I seemed to have a deep impression in my spirit that I could win, so I stepped over to one side of the store and breathed a prayer: "Oh, Lord, if I win it, I will bless others by paying my tithes on it." The figure *307* dropped into my spirit; I thought about it, but wrote down *309.*

Early Sunday morning as we were getting ready for Sunday school, there was a knock at the door. I said to my husband, "Answer the door, Honey; that is the man to tell you I won the flour!" And it was. . . . He said, "Are you Reverend Goodwin?" My husband replied, "Yes, I am." He said, "It was you, Mrs. Goodwin. The flour actually weighed 307 pounds, and you put down 309. That was the nearest number to it." We had biscuits galore for a long time.

—*Carmen Thacker Goodwin*
1992

Lord, thank You for the many ways You supply my needs, even the unusual ones. Keep my eyes open to them. In Jesus' name. Amen.

Springtime and Harvest (Broken Arrow, OK: Carmen Thacker Goodwin, 1992).

Day 4
Lead the Christ Life

READ 1 THESSALONIANS 5:14–24

Perhaps you have children. Are you living the Christ life before them? They may want to attend worldly amusements. Yield to them once or twice, and soon you will have no control over them. They have become acquainted with others who are leading them step by step away from Christ. They will not go to Sunday school or church. You see, you have made a mistake by yielding to them. Pray for them. Dear mothers, live the Christ life before your children. Teach them how to pray from their infancy. When they grow up, they will very seldom depart from it.

—*Sister Mary Canfield*
August 1922

Lord, thank You that Your Spirit empowers me to lead the Christ life before my children. Teach me, Lord, to teach them Your ways, and help me to model Christ always. In Jesus' name. Amen.

Taken from *Word and Work*.

Day 5

Free in Jesus

READ JOHN 8:36; 18:32; LUKE 13:12

Woman, be free! Jesus sets you free. When the Son makes you free, you are free indeed!

If you have been terrorized or censored by religious rulers; if tradition has you bent and bound; turn to Jesus. When you make contact with Him, your shackles will dissolve whether they are religious, psychological, physical, or spiritual. Be free, in the name of Jesus.

Jesus sets you free from negative thoughts, from guilt, from self-condemnation, from feelings of inferiority, timidity, fear, anxiety, and depression. Jesus sets you free from alcoholism and from drugs. When you are made whole by Jesus, your desires, thoughts, and habits change. Religion cannot change you. Jesus can, and does, because He gives you a new life—His life.

Woman, you are loosed from your shackles. Be free, in Jesus' name!

—*Daisy Washburn Osborn*
1991

Lord, thank You for setting me free! In Jesus' name. Amen.

Women and Self-Esteem (Tulsa, OK: OSFO Publishers, 1991).

Weekend

The Transformed Life

READ 2 CORINTHIANS 5:16–21

A young prostitute came to one of our meetings. She had sold her body to support her drug habit. She had been in and out of prison, but that had never changed her. A leopard cannot change its spots, it is said. But when she heard the gospel, she discovered new purpose for her life. She accepted Jesus Christ as her personal Savior. Her life was completely transformed, and she set out on a mission of love to lead depraved human beings to Jesus.

What a transformation takes place when a life is touched by Jesus! He forgives, heals, and restores in just a moment of time. Religion cannot do this for you, but Jesus can and will.

—*Daisy Washburn Osborn*
1991

Father, thank You for transforming my life by the finished work of Jesus at the cross. Now use me to bring that message of transformation to others. In Jesus' name. Amen.

Women and Self-Esteem (Tulsa, OK: OSFO Publishers, 1991).

Part 4—
IV
Fall

. . . a time

to pluck what is planted . . .

—*Ecclesiastes 3:2,* NKJV

Week 40—Day 1

Humility

READ PROVERBS 22:4; 1 PETER 5:5–9

Humility is perfect quietness of heart.

It is to have no trouble.

It is never to be fretted or vexed or irritated, or sore or disappointed.

It is to expect nothing, to wonder at nothing that is done to me, to feel nothing done against me.

It is to be at rest when nobody praises me, and when I am blamed or despised.

It is to have a blessed home in the Lord, where I can go in and shut the door, and kneel to my Father in secret, and am at peace as in a deep sea of calmness when all around and above are in trouble.

—*Item from* The Christian Evangel
November 1918

Lord, thank You for the gift of humility. Please keep me humble before You. In Jesus' name. Amen.

Day 2
Plague in St. Louis

READ ISAIAH 40:28–31

As I write, this is the third Sunday when all places of worship in Springfield have been closed on account of the plague, permitted by God, over our whole country, called the Spanish Influenza. I know that in other districts the same conditions prevail. Surely God is letting His children find out how even now how much they have of Him in their lives.

How much are we depending on each other for spiritual food? Does our pastor do most of our thinking and Bible reading and praying for us at the meetings we have been accustomed to attending? Or are we in the place spiritually where we can live in direct touch with God for the supply of our every need? Surely we need the prayer closet as never before, and as we wait before the Lord there, our strength will be renewed, and the Spirit of God will teach us things He desires us to know.

—*Alice Rowlands Frodsham*
November 1918

Lord, even in the valleys You are teaching me to trust You! Teach me what I need to learn. In Jesus' name. Amen.

"Secret Service Work," *The Christian Evangel.*

Day 3

In Times of Trial

READ 1 CORINTHIANS 3:8–11

How God makes us long, as He makes Himself so real to us in these everyday trials and emergencies, that every tried and anxious child of His may know the blessed rest there is in this secret service work. How it leads us into a deeper life of union with Him, so that He lets us be fellow-laborers with Him, and we really do cooperate with Jesus in the intercessory work He is doing on the throne. He communicates to us His plans, not only for our own lives, but we pray with Him for His whole body, which is the church.

As you, dear one, read this, unite with me, that I might be kept true and humble in all tests He may see fit to put me through until He comes. Yours, sheltered under the blood of Jesus, and believing in the power of His name—

—Alice Rowlands Frodsham
November 1918

Lord, thank You for revealing Yourself so powerfully in the midst of every trial, and for being very near and real to me. In Jesus' name. Amen.

"Secret Service Work," *The Christian Evangel.*

Day 4

Women of Prayer

READ 2 CHRONICLES 7:14; JAMES 4:6–10

An entry in Mrs. Dabney's journal:

The Lord has commanded me to call the women to prayer everywhere. I am praying that He will call two thousand especially, who will make the sacrifice and pray through to His glory. He has led me to call them to prayer at four o'clock in the morning. About three hundred and fifty assembled at three-thirty A.M. When I arrived at four o'clock, the Lord was in His temple, visiting His children with blessings. The saints cried to be led out with me into this Garden of Prayer. His presence filled the room. Everyone was overshadowed. In a great way the Lord poured His oil upon our heads. I heard the Spirit crying for souls to be revived and renewed and that they might not only be swimming in a river but out in the ocean of prayer.

—*Mrs. E. J. Dabney*
June 1940

Lord, thank You that You are still calling me to be a woman of prayer. Empower me, lead me, use me to pray that Your will is accomplished on earth, as it is in heaven. In Jesus' name. Amen.

An entry from the diary of E. J. Dabney, in "What It Means to Pray Through," *The Pentecostal Evangel.*

Day 5

What the Devil Fears

READ ACTS 26:16–18

The devil fears nothing like prayer. He knows that if he can break our communication with God, he has cut us off from all power. Hence, he sentinels the gateway of prayer with his seducing agents. He deadens the spiritual sensibilities, hatches excuses, makes evasions in the mind, causes us to suddenly grow dull and drowsy and indolent, and in a thousand other ways he works untiringly to keep us from getting hold of God in earnest prayer.

He engineers strange circumstances to keep us from our knees. He incites a false zeal and, in a multitude of church activities, crowds out prayer. To the degree that he succeeds in causing us to neglect prayer, he has won the day. Our victory comes in arousing and stirring up all the faculties of taking hold of God in the combats of prayer.

—*Sarah Elias Foulkes*
October 1936

Lord, stir me to prayer that I may be Your instrument to strike continual fear in the devil! Keep me covered in Your blood and give me the grace and fortitude to pray always. In Jesus' name. Amen.

"Revival Follows Prayer," *The Pentecostal Evangel.*

Weekend

Stand Still

READ EXODUS 14:13; 2 CHRONICLES 20:15, 17

The battle raged, the cannon roared:
I stood, to see the fight—
And lo, behold, I saw the Lord
Revealed, before my sight.
'Twas He who fought and won that day;
'Twas He who gave the word:
"Stand still, My child. Stand still, I say."
And yet another word I heard,
'Twas only this: "Obey."

—*Item from* The Pentecostal Evangel
August 1936

Father, thank You that Your instructions to me are as simple as the single word, "Obey!" I choose to obey You, now and always. In Jesus' name. Amen.

Week 41—Day 1

Angelic Protection

READ PSALM 34

One time in Africa thirty medicine men gathered to put a curse on a missionary and his family. It was a thirty-day contest between the medicine men and Jehovah God. The missionary, for some reason, said that he could not leave his station and call for help, so he decided to stay there and fight it out. The medicine men did put every type of curse on the man and his children. His children did get sick—but they prayed through together and the children became well again.

The medicine men were so desperate; they couldn't fail. The last night of the thirty-day contest, the men came with their torches to burn down the grass huts, and to burn out the missionary. What did they meet? Tall men in white garments with great swords drawn so that they could not break through. Prevailing prayer—what a power there is in intercession. It is a great weapon in spiritual warfare.

—Mrs. Gertrude Reidt
1986

Lord, thank You for the powerful protection of Your angelic host! In Jesus' name. Amen.

The Significance of Intercession (Wilford H. Reidt, 1986).

Day 2
An Angelic Bodyguard

READ ACTS 27:1–25

A lady missionary wrote: "During the awful night when looting was taking place and dangers surrounded the compound, not only were the praying band of Christians untouched, but a wonderful thing happened."

The previous night she had a very bad attack of malaria, and for a time the onslaught of the enemy was terrific. Those around said, "What will you do when the looters come here? What about these promises you have been trusting to when the firing begins?" She turned to Jesus, saying, "Lord, I have been teaching these people all these years to hold to Thy promises, and if they fail now I shall never be able to open my mouth again. I must just go home." Awful things were happening all around . . . but the mission compound was untouched.

In the morning neighbors asked, "Who were those four people, quietly watching from the top of your house all night long?" When told that no one had watched from the housetop, they refused to believe it: "We saw them with our own eyes!"

"Then they were told that God had sent His angel-guards to protect us."

—*Item from* The Pentecostal Evangel
February 1927

Lord, even in the midst of dangers, thank You that Your angels camp around me because I am Your child. In Jesus' name. Amen.

Day 3

Darwin's Last Days

READ HEBREWS 11

How many of Darwin's disciples know of his last days? Lady Hope of Northfield, England, sent this item:

"I asked to go and sit with the well-known professor, Charles Darwin . . . almost bedridden for some months before he died. He was sitting on a couch near a large window, wearing a soft embroidered dressing gown of rather a rich purple shade. Propped up by pillows, he was gazing out on a far-stretching scene of woods which glowed in the light of one of those marvelous sunsets which are the beauty of Kent and Surrey. He waved his hand toward the window as he pointed out the scene beyond, while in the other hand he held an open Bible, which he was always studying. 'What are you reading now?' I asked.

"'Hebrews,' he answered. 'Still Hebrews—the Royal Book, I call it. Isn't it grand?'

"He seemed greatly distressed as he said: 'I was a young man with unformed ideas. I threw out queries, suggestions, wondering all the time over everything; and to my astonishment the ideas took like wildfire. People made a religion of them. Oh, if I could only undo it!'"

—Item in The Pentecostal Evangel
February 1927

Lord, thank You for revealing Yourself to Charles Darwin in his last days. Thank You for Your mercy that extends to all. Amen.

Day 4
God's Blank Checks

READ JEREMIAH 33:2–2; LUKE 11:9–10

Are you using your check book? Jesus has said, "Ye shall ask and I will do." He has signed His name to a vast check book full of blank checks and has put one into the hand of each of His blood-washed ones, saying, "Fill in the checks and present them at the throne of grace. I will honor every one you present in the name of Jesus, and will give you each time you draw on Me more than you call for!"

"Call unto Me and I will answer thee, and show thee great and mighty things, which thou knowest not."

Cash your checks! You can draw on the eternal promises of God!

> I have a never-failing bank,
> Well filled with golden store;
> No other bank contains so much
> That can enrich the poor.
> Sometimes my banker smiling says,
> "Why don't you oft'ner come?"
> And when I draw a little note,
> "Why not a larger one?"

—*Elizabeth Sisson*
December 1923

Lord, thank You that You are my banker; thank You for giving me my own heavenly check book from which to draw out answers to Your abundant promises! Amen.

"Prayer," *The Pentecostal Evangel.*

Day 5
Get in Touch With God

READ EPHESIANS 5:18–21

When you want to get in touch with the God of power, go into a room for several days, shut the door behind you, and spend time alone with the Bible and God. When you tell God you are not going to come out until you have all that He has for you in Jesus, God is going to move!

He will see your persistence, and the wine of God will flow through your life. People will come to hear you because you have been ministering to the Lord. You will begin to see people really touched by the hand of the Savior, not by the message alone, but by the person of the Holy Spirit. If you take a brand and hold it in the fire, it is going to get red hot. Begin to abide. Begin to read the Word. Begin to minister to Him. Start doing the basic, simple things that Jesus taught.

Being filled with praise and worship to the Lord should be a result of walking in the fullness of the Holy Spirit. Paul, in the fifth chapter of Ephesians, tells us that if we are walking in the Spirit, there will be manifest results.

—*Roxanne Brandt*
1973

Lord, I want to get in touch with You! Lead me in Your Word and guide me in the quietness of prayer. Take me higher, Lord! In Jesus' name. Amen.

Ministering to the Lord (Springdale, PA: Whitaker House, 1973).

Weekend

The Only Remedy

READ PSALM 88

From the journal of Sister Dabney:

Prayer is the only remedy for this day of ills and chills. In the midst of it all, thank God I have found a place, way out in the Spirit upon the mountain, where a praying woman can go and be with God.

Come, dear one, with me out there where Jesus will intercede through you and deliver many sinners through your prayers. If you will follow me into this field of prayer you will thank me for urging you to give your life to pray sinners through to God. He has praying ground to give you which has never been possessed by anybody. He has praying hills and mountains that nobody has ever asked Him for. Your feet can stand on a new height every day and night.

—*Mrs. E. J. Dabney*
1940

Lord, I follow You up to that place far out in the Spirit, high upon on the mountain, where I can pray. Give me a heart for intercession. In Jesus' name. Amen.

"What It Means to Pray Through," *The Pentecostal Evangel.*

Week 42—Day 1
Fasting

READ MATTHEW 6:16

In history, fasting was usually called in times of sorrow, mourning, or great affliction. This was the Old Testament way. Until the time of Moses, fasting was never mentioned in the Bible. Jesus set no pattern, because He did not want us to get into a mold regarding fasting, which would make it a religious requirement, and thus not of God.

Nature itself will put a fast on you when it is entirely necessary. Fasting is not simply abstinence from good; a total fast is to fast from all pleasures that take time and thought away from God. When you truly fast, you'd better leave everything alone, leave all your side-issues that you like so well, for not to do so is to not fast before God's eyes. Fasting must be done in sincerity and truth, not as before men but as before God. Those who openly fast have their reward; they received the acclaim of men but not of God.

Fasting should never appear as an act of hardship but as an act of joy. We need to leave it up to the Holy Spirit as to when to lead us on to a fast.

—*Jeanne Wilkerson*
n.d.

Father, thank You for leading me by Your Spirit to occasional fasting, when prayers are intensified. Pour out more grace when it's time to fast and pray. In Jesus' name. Amen.

Adapted from an audiocassette titled "Fasting and Prayer."

Day 2
Leading by Serving

READ MATTHEW 23:11–12; LUKE 16:13

Anyone wanting to be in leadership must learn to serve. Jesus introduced leadership as serving, and servanthood as the mark of greatness. He gave us the key to true humility, and the formula for genuine meekness.

Jesus was meek. He was gentle. He was a servant. But He was—and is—the greatest of all leaders. We can risk following His teaching and His example. In doing so, He gives us the quality of mind necessary to become a servant.

Choose to serve. Take the initiative. Whatever you do, do it with a servant's mind and heart. You will be astonished at the change this will bring to your life as a woman follower of Christ.

—*Daisy Washburn Osborn*
1991

Lord, teach me to serve. In Jesus' name. Amen.

Women and Self-Esteem (Tulsa, OK: OSFO Publishers, 1991).

Day 3

Fervency!

READ ACTS 18:24–28

The reason so many prayers are fruitless is the lack of fervency. We must be fervent in Spirit, and above all, have faith in God.

> This faith in the dark,
> Pursuing its mark;
> Thru many sharp trials of love,
> Is the sorrowful waste,
> That is to be passed
> In the way to the Canaan above.
>
> —*Madame Guyon*

Persistent prayer accompanied by faith subdues the invincible and prevails with omnipotence. Hallelujah!

—*Mrs. Ida McCoy*
n.d.

Lord, help me to learn fervent, prevailing prayer! In Jesus' name. Amen.

Neglected Themes and Helpful Hints (n.p., n.d.).

Day 4

A Woman's Desires

READ JEREMIAH 29:11–14

God wants you, as His royal daughter, to realize that within you is the possibility to shed the cloak of failure, escape the negative syndrome of discouragement, break with the demoralizing dogmas of defeat, get out of the boredom of conformity, and go for life in abundance—whether the majority of women do it or not.

No woman believer should be subordinated in life without personal means, material achievements, self-pride of personal enterprise, and self-esteem and the dignity of realizing her personal success. Ascend to your desires, and dare to tackle life. Harness the abilities of God within you. Embrace the fact that as He is, so are you in this world.

—*Daisy Washburn Osborn*
1991

Lord, I choose to rise up into all that You have planned for my life. I choose to tackle life! In Jesus' name. Amen.

New Life for Women (Tulsa, OK: OSFO Publishers, 1991).

Day 5
Yearning Power

READ PSALM 73:23–28

A woman's *yearning power* is more important than her *earning power!*

Women who succeed in life focus on the direction they desire to go and refuse the restrictive-limit mentality which society tends to impose upon them.

Recognize that God is at work within you, helping you to want what He wants, to desire what He desires. I have published these vital ideas to encourage you, as a woman, and to motivate you to never again allow people, or systems, or traditions, or culture to discredit your dreams, dampen your ambitions, or suppress your aspirations.

—*Daisy Washburn Osborn*
1991

Lord, I yearn for more of You, and to be used by You during these End Times. Empower me by Your Spirit and reveal to me what it is You intend for me to do. In Jesus' name. Amen.

New Life for Women (Tulsa, OK: OSFO Publishers, 1991).

Weekend

Praying Through

READ GENESIS 28:10–16

If you need to pray through about something, stay in the presence of God, in prayer, until you get through to Him. God will reveal Himself. He will talk to you . . . but maybe not the first time; I should say not!

Just lately, I had to have a *yes* or *no* from God. I could have made my own plans and said, "This is what I want and this is what I'm going to do." But I can't operate like that; I want to hear God. I have to know that I am moving in the will of God, and when I know I'm in God's will He will give me His Word and anoint me by His Spirit. Then I can get somewhere with God.

Because I had to have a word from God (and the devil knew it), I said, "I don't care how long it takes! I'm going to stay here! I absolutely refuse to give an answer to this question until I hear from God!"

—*Hattie Hammond*
n.d.

Lord, that's how badly I need a word from You! I'm going to stay before You in prayer until it comes. In Jesus' name. Amen.

Audiocassette titled "How to Pray," from a chapel service at Christ for the Nations.

Week 43—Day 1
However Long It Takes

READ PSALM 55:16–22

I got up in the morning, had a little breakfast, and went to prayer. I prayed all day long and all that night. I got a little weary toward morning and just lay on the davenport—a kind of altar at my house! As soon as I got up I started to pray again, and I prayed all that day too. I prayed all the next night until, between two and three in the morning, Jesus came into the room!

At that moment of time there was a release of the whole panorama of His will. Every cell of my body, my brain, my heart, my flesh knew what God was saying . . . what He wanted.

That wasn't the first time it had taken days and nights in His presence. But that's how you pray through! Don't wander around in confusion! Pray through!

—*Hattie Hammond*
n.d.

Father, thank You for teaching me how to pray through! In Jesus' name. Amen.

Audiocassette titled "How to Pray," from a chapel service at Christ for the Nations.

Day 2
Christ Crowned Within

READ PSALM 11

When Christ is crowned within, we depart from evil and seek after peace, as much as possible, with all men. To have Christ crowned within is a joy unspeakable and full of glory; it is unspeakable because it is like a well of water springing up within our souls. It is joy that is inexhaustible. No matter how fast troubles may come, or how deeply we may be plunged into sorrow, there is still that deep settle peace within our souls. Why? Because Christ is crowned within, and He is having His way with us.

When we have Christ crowned within, enthroned within our hearts, He anoints our eyes with eye salve that we may have a clearer vision of heavenly things. He also takes us to deeper depths with Him. Therefore, we are able to walk in the path that He Himself has marked out for us, and by so doing we shall be able to keep ourselves unspotted from the world.

—*Sara Holland*
February 1924

Lord, thank You that Christ is crowned within my heart! Amen.

"Christ Crowned Within," *Word and Work.*

Day 3
The Taxi Ride

READ PROVERBS 31:26; 2 PETER 1:4–8

A certain woman asked me to go with her to pray for a sick friend. I felt led to go, so the woman said she would come by in a taxi and take me to see her friend. When we got into the cab, the woman went on and on, telling me how wonderful Jesus was to her, and how wonderful it was to be a Christian. She told me that she had had many dreams, visions, and revelations.

She had given the taxi driver instructions, but I'm sure he was as taken as I was, just listening to the woman's fabulous stories, so he sailed right past the corner where he should have turned. We went way past our turnoff. The woman then tore into that driver, saying, "I gave you instructions!" She went on and on, and really let him have it. I was so embarrassed that I wanted to get out of the cab—fast. I can still hear that taxi driver say, "If that's dreams, visions, and revelations, forget it! I don't want that!"

—Hattie Hammond
n.d.

Lord, forgive me for the times my behavior toward others has not measured up to my claims of Christianity. Use this story to make me more aware of my treatment of others. In Jesus' name. Amen.

Audiocassette titled "Give Me Your Heart," from a chapel service at Christ for the Nations.

$\mathscr{D}ay\ 4$
$\mathscr{S}hadrach,\ \mathscr{M}eshach,\ and\ \mathscr{A}bednego$

READ ACTS 17:24–28

God is our home. He is our Source. He is our beginning and our ending. We come from God, and we will return to Him. God Himself taught me this. When I was a little girl I loved goldfish. I had a beautiful bowl of them. These three unusual goldfish, I named Shadrach, Meshach, and Abednego. Their habitat was the goldfish bowl, which was kept in the living room. They were surrounded by water, where they lived and moved and had their being.

God the Father said to me, "That's the way I want you to live—in Me." His banner over us is love; He is a wall of fire around us, and the glory in the midst of us. So there He is—God over us, all around us, in us. He wants us to live the God consciousness, surrounded by Him, where we live and move and have our being—like Shadrach, Meshach, and Abednego swimming around in their goldfish bowl!

—*Hattie Hammond*
n.d.

Lord, thank You for reminding me that in You I live
and move and have my being! In Jesus' name. Amen.

Audiocassette titled "Agelessness," from a chapel service at Christ for the Nations.

Day 5
Don't Stop Now!

READ 1 CORINTHIANS 2:9–10; HEBREWS 6:1

Many dear children of the Lord stop short at conversion and consecration, and fail to continue on to receive the Holy Spirit. Also, many who have received the Holy Spirit stop short of going on and receiving all the Spirit has to bestow in the gifts, fruits, and deeper revelations which were lost in the Dark Ages.

We do not see the gifts and the fruit as yet matured, perhaps, but as we pray and trust and follow the leadings of the Holy Spirit, He will divide every man severally as He will, and cause the gifts and fruit to be more visible in our midst.

—*Mattie Crawford*
1926

> Lord, I'm going on with You until the fruit of the Spirit and the gifts of the Spirit are developed by You to the degree that You would have them come forth. Use them to Your glory! Amen.

The Baptism of the Holy Spirit (Los Angeles, CA: Publication and Executive Office, 1926).

Weekend

All Shall Be Restored

READ JOEL 2

All the years that were lost shall be restored! God is still prophesying that to His children. Dear ones, there is yet land to be possessed. Let the fruit of love be wrought out in your life, along with joy, peace, long-suffering, goodness, meekness, faith, meekness, temperance. Let us regain our long-standing inheritance, as recorded in God's Word, for Jesus is coming soon . . , very soon . . . for His perfect, waiting Bride. He is coming for His unblemished and perfected people, uncontaminated with the false leaven of the world, old Rome, or the ecclesiasticism of the day.

Let us watch and be exceedingly careful that we do not fall into the same snares into which many others, formerly used and blessed by the Lord, have fallen—snares of coldness, pride, formality, iron-clad creeds, and organizations. Let us keep from building walls of tradition about ourselves and so failing to recognize the other members of the Lord's body, "for by one Spirit we are all baptized into one body." God will step over manmade walls and call out and take out His people. He will not permit His church to stop short of full restoration!

—*Mattie Crawford*
1926

I praise You for Your promise to restore the years that the enemy has eaten from my life. Do it, Lord! Amen.

The Baptism of the Holy Spirit (Los Angeles, CA: Publication and Executive Office, 1926).

Week 44—Day 1
God's Upward Call

READ ISAIAH 26:16; 1 THESSALONIANS 4:16

The next upward call of God is His call to the dead in Christ. They will be first to hear the "upward call." Oh, how wonderful that will be! Redeemed ones filling the air with song and rejoicing, called up to meet their Lord in the air.

The next call shall be heart, not only by the resurrected saints, but by those also who are alive and remain until that great event. The quick and the dead shall stand together, and they shall all hear His gracious words, "Come up hither!"

—Mrs. E. A. Sexton
February 1918

Jesus, I wait for You. Maranatha! Amen.

The Pentecostal Holiness Advocate.

Day 2

Nearer and Nearer

READ LUKE 21

We are drawing nearer and nearer to that momentous day of our deliverance! Every tick of the clock reduces our time of watching and waiting. Soon our patience and faithfulness will be rewarded. Our adversary will do his utmost to hinder our preparation for the Rapture or to keep that number as small as possible, but in spite of all hindrances to thwart the saints there will be a glorious ascension of bloodwashed overcomers, clothed with immortality, transformed into the image of their Lord and radiant with his righteousness, who will hear the Lord's "upward call."

The world will know nothing about this call. Only the prepared saints will hear and understand. He is not due to come to the world until after the great tribulation. He will not plant His feet on the Mount of Olives until He comes with ten thousand of His saints to reign a thousand years. His "upward call" to the saints will be heard several years before He comes to reign. They shall rise, when He calls, and meet Him in the air. May God give us wisdom and understanding, for the time is short. It may be very soon that we shall hear the "upward call." It may be sooner than we think!

—*Mrs. E. A. Sexton*
February 1918

Lord, prepare me to meet You in the air. In Jesus' name. Amen.

Day 3

God's Viewpoint

READ LUKE 8:2; MARK 14:3–9

A young woman was saved in New York City, and has since become a great soulwinner. She had been a chemical dependent and a prostitute.

There were three pornographic cinemas, side by side, in a New York ghetto. The middle one was for sale. So, with money raised by Christians, it was purchased and gospel meetings began. Opposite the entrance were three hotels, managed by professional pimps for their prostitutes. That young woman—herself a reformed prostitute—chose that place to begin a new work for God. She had God's viewpoint of life, and others. She knew that she could only love and serve God by loving and serving others.

—*Daisy Washburn Osborn*
1991

Lord, use me to reach out to others. Forgive me for forgetting that to love You is to preach the gospel, and to serve. In Jesus' name. Amen.

Women and Self-Esteem (Tulsa, OK: OSFO Publishers, 1991).

Day 4
Broken Vows

READ PSALM 116:16–19

I would not want you to know the vows I have broken, and I would not want to know the vows you have broken. But I am glad that I can say that the Lord brought me to the old mourner's bench and caused me to see my broken vows. I cried out to God and paid my vows, and then the fire came sweeping over my soul. Ever since I have had a Pentecostal revival burning in my heart.

Our God never changes. He wants a people who will not break their covenant, who will not forsake their vows, but measure up to His standard, living a life that is holy and righteous before Him.

—Evangelist Emma Taylor
May 1936

Lord, thank You for reminding me that You are a God
of covenant. Forgive me for any broken vows, and keep
me faithful to You in covenant. In Jesus' name. Amen.

"Paying Our Vows," *The Pentecostal Evangel.*

Day 5

"He Sanctified Me!"

READ JOHN 17:13–19; ROMANS 15:16

We made our way to the mission on Azusa Street and found the people upon whom God had so copiously poured out His Spirit. I was not looking at the people. I was seeking more from the God of Israel. A man arose to his feet and said, "Hallelujah!" My soul responded, "God, I have heard from Heaven."

Before I left that place I had an interview with the minister in charge. I told him, "I am hungry for more of God and cannot find the satisfying portion." He looked into my face and said, "Sister, you have a wonderful case of salvation, but you need to be sanctified."

That following week I continually and earnestly sought God. I searched out the truths of His Word. Oh, how I hungered for that experience of sanctification. The next Friday when I returned to the services, the preacher stopped his preaching and said, "Somebody in this place wants something from God." I pushed the chairs away from in front of me and dropped upon my knees at the altar. The "fire" fell, and God sanctified me. Oh, it was marvelous.

—*Florence Crawford*
1965

Lord, I want more of You! Please fill me to overflowing with Your Spirit, and let the fire from heaven fall! In Jesus' name. Amen.

A Historical Account of the Apostolic Faith (Portland, OR: The Apostolic Faith Publishing House, 1965).

Weekend

A 1,000 Percent Return

READ MALACHI 3:10–12

Tithing is not a duty; it is a privilege. Giving is a part of worship. One-tenth belongs to God anyway; what you give above that is your offering.

The best investment in the world is an investment in the kingdom of God. It is giltedged, backed by all the resources of heaven, signed by the One who made the world, and the dividends of at least 1000 percent continue through all eternity.

—*Item from* Golden Grain
1932

Lord, thank You that the best returns in history are paid on my tithe! Bless and multiply the tithe, and use it to further Your kingdom. In Jesus' name. Amen.

Week 45—Day 1
Hold Fast

READ JAMES 5:14–15

We read in the fifth chapter of James that the prayer of faith will save the sick, and you readily say that God alone can forgive sin. Who is it that raises up the sick? You answer, "God," and yet when your friends and neighbors are sick for weeks and months and years, and the "arm of the flesh" has proved too short to help them, you do not think of applying to the Great Physician, with faith in His power and willingness to heal.

And when the Lord impresses upon the mind of one of His suffering children that "the prayer of faith shall save the sick," and leads them to send for one of God's faithful followers who is "holding fast to the profession of faith," and when he is anointed with oil and God answers that payer and raises up the sick one to His glory and praise, you are ready to call it all a humbug and close your eyes to the facts. O let those who believe in God's precious truths hold fast to the profession of their faith, not doubt His Word, put away all fear, lay aside all preconceived opinions, all traditions that have warped the mind, and *believe the whole gospel!*

—Mrs. Edward Mix
1881

Lord, thank You for the whole gospel, which includes healing and miracles. In Jesus' name. Amen.

"Holding Fast," *Triumphs of Faith.*

Day 2
A New Creature

READ 2 CORINTHIANS 5:17

This is one of the most important messages of your life: You are a new creature! Get it straightened out that Jesus is in you; you're a new creation, a new person. Get it straight that you are done with that old sin nature that you inherited from Adam. Your new life is Christ.

Look at Paul! We see it in him. There he was, out on the road to Damascus, struck to the ground by the power of God. When he got up out of the dust and said, "What happened to me?" he realized that the power of the Lord had changed him. Five minutes before, he had been on his way to murder Christians. Now, he was saying, "Lord, what will You have me do?" Paul had such a vision and understanding of the transformed life that he later wrote, "Christ liveth in me! I am crucified with Christ." This is the gospel message of Paul— the power we tell others about. We are new creatures—instruments of life to bring the life of Christ to the world.

—*Hattie Hammond*
n.d.

Lord, give me the vision and understanding of what it means to be transformed—changed by the power of the Holy Spirit into the image and likeness of Christ. In Jesus' name. Amen.

Audiocassette titled "Life-Bearers," from a chapel service at Christ for the Nations.

Day 3

A Maxim

READ PHILIPPIANS 3:7–14

Learn today the secret of never suffering loss in the soul by the sufferings of life—yea, rather, of always making them your greatest gain. Link them to God and to Jesus.

—*Item in* The Pentecostal Evangel
August 1936

Lord, thank You that You can bring growth and good out of suffering. Help me to count them as gain. In Jesus' name. Amen.

Day 4

Prayer and Faith

READ PSALM 119:10–18

The great intercessor, George Müller, once said, "Prayer and faith, the universal remedies against every want and every difficulty; and the nourishment of prayer and faith, God's Holy Word, have helped me over all difficulties. I never remember in all my Christian course, that I ever sincerely and patiently sought to know the will of God by the teaching of the Holy Ghost, through the instrumentality of the Word of God, but I have been always directed rightly."

We can get things from God if we will but pay the price. Too many are too lazy to wait, and others are in too much of a hurry. God has a bountiful storehouse of good things for His people. He is ready and willing to give us His best. Have we spent any time this week asking Him for anything of real spiritual value? Have we asked in faith, expecting an answer? Let us move forward on our knees to see what God will do for both the pulpit and the pew.

—*Beatrice V. Pannabecker*
August 1936

Lord, I move forward on my knees, in prayer, to discover what You have for me. In Jesus' name. Amen.

"Are You Getting Things From God?" *The Pentecostal Evangel.*

Day 5

Answering the Call

READ MARK 16:15–18

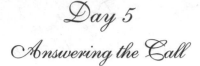

When someone asked a missionary if he liked his work in Africa, he replied: "Do I like this work? No; my wife and I do not like dirt. We have reasonably refined sensibilities. We do not like crawling into vile huts through goat refuse. We do not like association with ignorant, filthy, brutish people. *But is a man to do nothing for Christ he does not like?* God pity him, if not. Liking or disliking has nothing to do with it. We have orders to 'go,' and we go. Love constrains us."

Such a love begets the strength to do the "all things."

—*Item from* The Pentecostal Evangel
August 1936

Lord, I say yes to Your call; use me as You see fit, and help me to always remember that my motivation to serve You must be love. In Jesus' name. Amen.

Weekend

Words to Live By

READ ISAIAH 53

There are some things that become indelibly impressed upon one's mind, and will linger forever. Of all the statements I have heard in my thirty-five years the most wonderful of all and the one which I shall never forget, was that which my dear wife made when she said, *"If Jesus could stand it, surely I can."*

That was the phrase the Lord used to break down my opposition and my hatred of the Lord Jesus Christ.

—*Item from* The Pentecostal Evangel
August 1936

Lord, forgive me for forgetting that Jesus bore the burden for what I'm going through now. I'm sorry for complaining and for grumbling about my circumstances. Help me to fix my eyes afresh on Christ, and give Him glory for setting the perfect example. In Jesus' name. Amen.

Week 46—Day 1
Anointed to Preach Healing

READ PSALM 30

I received my anointing thirty-five years ago when God raised me up from the sick bed. God showed me that I must preach healing, and I told the people how God raised me up. After a while I was holding a meeting in Indiana, and worked nearly to death, sometimes nearly all night. The Spirit of the Lord came upon me; God was trying to show me that He wanted me to preach healing for the sick, but I was afraid it was the enemy. It seemed like presumption. Many souls would be saved through divine healing, and the devil knew it.

Healing is the great drawing card in the New Testament. Finally, I settled the question: I knew it was the Lord, and I said, "Whatever You want me to pray for someone, bring them to me, or take me to them, and I will do it."

—Maria Woodworth-Etter
1976

Lord, thank You for the anointing that breaks yokes—yokes that include sickness. Use me, Lord, to pray for the sick. In Jesus' name. Amen.

Signs and Wonders (Bartlesville, OK: Oak Tree Publications, Inc., 1976).

Day 2
Death Demon Conquered

READ JOHN 14:12

The following testimony is that of a woman who was raised from the dead when Sister Etter prayed for her:

"Last Friday I was very sick. I did not know what was the matter, but I went to church on the strength of Jesus, and then fainted. One of God's children laid hands on me and prayed. The sickness increased; I could not see and could not talk. Then I became unconscious. The people said I was dead: The pulse had ceased to beat and health was gone, eyes and jaws were set. When I recovered consciousness, Sister Etter was standing over me, rebuking the spirit of death. It seemed to me the smile of heaven was on her face, and such peace. I felt as if I was in the arms of Jesus."

Sister Etter said, "You are poisoned."

Those present that evening said Sister Etter had rebuked the spirit of death, and commanded the woman, "Rise up!"

—*Mrs. J. C. Brewer*
1914

Lord, thank You that You promised we would do great works in Your name. Thank You for the resurrection power of the Holy Spirit. In Jesus' name. Amen.

Taken from *Signs and Wonders* by Mrs. M. Woodworth-Etter, (Bartlesville, OK: Oak Tree Publications, Inc., 1976).

Day 3

Invitation to a Wedding

READ MATTHEW 25:1–13

Jesus is giving you an invitation to a wedding. Will you accept it? Will you be one of the little flock? The angels are holding back the four winds—they are crying. Shall we let loose? No, not until we have sealed the servants of God with the seal of the living God in the forehead.

Perhaps you are a servant of God. You want to be sealed—baptized in the flesh, filled with new life. And some of these days, we will burst these bonds and go up to meet the Lord in the air. You that love Jesus will be tested. Make up your mind that you will stand on the Rock and if the whole world should leave, you won't, because Christ will be sufficient. It is going to be harder every day, even among the people of God. Keep under the blood, keep white, keep holy, keep pure, and God will give us wisdom.

—Maria Woodworth-Etter
n.d.

Lord, I accept Your wedding invitation! Purify me and make me ready to become Your Bride. In Jesus' name. Amen.

Holy Ghost Sermons (Self-published, n.d.).

Day 4
Be Careful What You Say

READ MATTHEW 12:31–32

There has never been a time since the early church when there was so much danger of people committing the unpardonable sin as there is today, since the Pentecostal fire has girdled the earth and thousands have received the baptism in the Holy Ghost. This is backed up with signs and wonders and divers operations of the Spirit. When men and women come in contact with this work of the Holy Ghost, feeling His presence, hearing His words, seeking His works, there is the danger lest they condemn the power and condemn God's servants.

How often we have heard ministers say, "Oh, it is the work of the devil!" Now, you hear what God says about it: They are speaking against the Holy Ghost!

—*Maria Woodworth-Etter*
August 1913

> *Lord, thank You for the Holy Spirit. Help me to properly discern His work and words, and to be careful what I say about those things I don't understand. In Jesus' name. Amen.*

"Blasphemy Against the Holy Ghost," *The Latter Rain Evangel.*

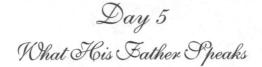

Day 5
What His Father Speaks

READ JOHN 14

In order to guard against committing the unpardonable sin, we must know a little of who the Holy Ghost is. He could not come until Christ was glorified. Christ was on earth in His human body for only a short time, but at Pentecost He came through the Holy Spirit—to stay. Jesus said that when the Holy Ghost should come whom the Father would send in His name, "He shall abide with you forever." And we were promised that He would not speak of Himself, but that which He hears His Father speak He will say. Oh, I love the Holy Ghost because He is always witnessing to Jesus, and He comes to bring us power.

He is the Comforter, the Spirit of Truth, who shall abide forever. He brings all things to our remembrance. We are so forgetful in our natural state, but we have a spiritual mind and God writes His Word there and the Holy Spirit brings these messages back to us at the right time—a message to this one in sin, to that one in sorrow, encouraging the weak and helping the strong with some message from heaven, always pointing us to Jesus, the great Burden-Bearer.

—*Maria Woodworth-Etter*
August 1913

> *Lord, thank You for the Holy Spirit. Please pour out more of Your Spirit, as You teach me to walk in the Spirit daily. In Jesus' name. Amen.*

"Blasphemy Against the Holy Ghost," *The Latter Rain Evangel.*

Weekend

Stir Up the Gift!

READ 2 TIMOTHY 1:1–7

Paul said to Timothy, "Stir up the gift of God which is in thee."

If there is any gift God is showing you that you ought to have, you can receive it by the laying on of hands. It is not so much what you say about the baptism in the Holy Spirit, but what they see you have. We can talk until we are hoarse and they won't be convinced, but the power of God convinces them. Don't wait for manifestations before you go forth and do something. When you are weakest, then you are strong. Let us go out and work miracles. Then the people will glorify God.

—*Maria Woodworth-Etter*
August 1913

Lord, show me the gifts You desire for me to have. Help me to stir up the gifts and use them, to Your glory. In Jesus' name. Amen.

"Blasphemy Against the Holy Ghost," *The Latter Rain Evangel.*

Week 47—Day 1
I Am Not Ashamed

READ ROMANS 1:16–17

I have tested the truth; I know it is of God. How can we help talking of the things we have seen? I have seen things by the Spirit, and in visions. I have seen Jesus, heavens open, the Marriage Supper, hosts of angels, the glory of God. I have seen them, glory to God! I know what I am telling you. I know Jesus lives and is standing by my side, more truly than I know you are here. These things are verities.

I am not ashamed of the Gospel of Christ! When a weak woman comes here to tell you what strong men ought to have told you, what are you going to think about it? I say these things are true; and when people say they are foolishness and fanaticism, dare they attempt to prove it by the Word? I dare them to do it! When they can prove the Holy Ghost has been taken out of the world, away from God's people, I am ready to go to prison—not before.

—*Maria Woodworth-Etter*
n.d.

Lord, thank You for the Holy Spirit, and for signs and wonders. Increase the power of the Holy Spirit within me as You increase the Spirit's outpouring in my life. In Jesus' name. Amen.

Holy Ghost Sermons (Self-published, n.d.).

Day 2
You Have Free Will

READ REVELATION 3:20–22

You are a free-will agent; you must decide for yourself. Jesus has opened the way, and He is holding the gate open wide for you just now. O come just now. Never, never blame Jesus, or say that He sent you to hell, for if you refuse to be saved and enter in, you send yourself there; He has done His part. How He will help you and carry you through if you will only let Him. Just now, wherever you are, He is whispering: "Behold, I stand at your heart's door and knock." Open to Him just now. Say, "I will rise and go unto my Father." Today is the day of salvation. You have no lease of tomorrow. Come just now.

Angels are lingering near,
Prayers rise from hearts so dear,
O wanderer, come.

EDITOR'S NOTE: *This is the sort of impassioned altar call that Aimee Semple McPherson was so famous for issuing during her dynamic ministry.*

—*Aimee Semple McPherson*
November 1923

Lord, thank You for Calvary. I use my free will to line up with Your perfect will for my life. Lead me there, Lord. In Jesus' name. Amen.

This Is That (Self-published, 1923). Used by permission of the Heritage Department of the Foursquare Gospel.

Day 3
Take No Thought

READ MATTHEW 6:25–34

I remember when Jesus called me to go and preach the gospel, my darling little mother has always stood back of me, God bless her. When I was going out into the work, Mother said, "Aimee (I was about to marry the evangelist under whom I had been converted), who is going to buy your things? You know Robert hasn't any salary."

"Mother, I know it."

"Who is going to buy your shoes, your dresses, and look after you?"

"I don't know, but I will ask the Lord about it." I prayed before my open Bible; Jesus spoke from the pages: "Child, take no thought of what you shall eat, drink, or put on. The Lord knows you have need of these things. Consider the lilies, they toil not, neither do they spin, and yet Solomon in all his glory was not arrayed like one of these." I said, "Oh, thank You, Jesus!" And from that day to this I have never worried one second about what I had to eat, drink, and wear.

—*Aimee Semple McPherson*
1923

> *Lord, I thank You for Your care of me. Help me to take*
> *no thought of what I will eat, drink, or wear, but in all*
> *things to ask You for Your marvelous provision. In*
> *Jesus' name. Amen.*

This Is That (Self-published, 1923). Used by permission of the Heritage Department of the Foursquare Gospel.

Day 4

Though They Be Few

READ MATTHEW 18:18–20

The number of those who press on all the way are often pathetically few:

—But *one* Noah, just and devout, when the floods came down!

—But *one* Lot in Sodom, and even his wife turned back!

—But *one* interceding Abraham, to whom God could reveal this coming catastrophe, and who could pray for the city's deliverance.

—But *one* Joseph in Egypt, who stood for the true God, and there declared His Word!

—But *one* Moses to lead the children of Israel forth!

—But *one* Daniel in the kingdom, who dared stand for the right and be true to the courage of his convictions!

Thanks be to God, however, the number need never be lessened to one! We need never walk alone, for even they who view afar off will ever see "two" going to the Jordan.

—*Aimee Semple McPherson*
1923

Lord, thank You that as I press on, You are with me every step of the way! In Jesus' name. Amen.

This Is That (Self-published, 1923). Used by permission of the Heritage Department of the Foursquare Gospel.

Day 5
The Rod of Moses

READ EXODUS 4:1–5

Moses went to Egypt to lead the people out. Before Pharaoh, he threw down his rod and it became a live serpent. The magicians said they had the same power, so they threw their rods down, and their rods also became serpents. But one act was of God and the other was of the devil. Moses did not get scared and run away; he knew God, and would not have run if all the serpents in Egypt had come before him.

Moses stood his ground, and I admire him for it. I do not like a coward. What was the result? Moses' serpent swallowed up the others, head and tail! There was nothing left of them. Those who are trying to overthrow the power of God and substitute something else will also have a day of judgment. The time is coming when the almighty God will manifest His power, and they, too, will be swallowed up.

—*Maria Woodworth-Etter*
1921

> *Lord, thank You that Your power is always greater than the power of any counterfeit or demonic substitute. Help me to stand my ground, in the power of the Holy Spirit, against the forces of darkness. In Jesus' name. Amen.*

Spirit-Filled Sermons (Self-published, 1921).

Weekend

The Offering of Praise

READ PSALM 9; REVELATION 8:3

You may have but little gold or silver—a little of this world's goods to offer—but there is no excuse for being sparing or miserly with His praises.

Heap up His praises upon the glowing altar of your soul, and pile His adoration atop of that, crown Him with glory, laud, and magnify His name until His burning praises rise as a sweet-smelling savor to be caught in the golden censer of the angel who offers unto the Lord the prayers of all saints upon the golden altar.

Let your heart be tuned up until it shall be as a harp of a thousand strings swept with melody by the fingers of the Holy Spirit if you have hung your harp on the willow tree, if the rust of coldness or self or formality has formed upon the strings, or if they are broken or out of tune.

Let the Holy Spirit tune up each string until again the music will spring forth at His slightest touch.

—*Aimee Semple McPherson*
n.d.

Lord, I choose to praise You. Let my offering of praise rise up from deep within, as incense before Your throne. In Jesus' name. Amen.

Adapted from a sermon titled "Praising the Lord." Used by permission of the Heritage Department of the Foursquare Gospel.

Week 48—Day 1
The Great I Am

READ EXODUS 15:26; HEBREWS 13:8

Sunset! Empty wheelchairs—deserted stretchers— piled-up crutches, thinning lines still pressing altar-ward. Happy couples departing arm in arm, cripples trying out newfound limbs, and a wilted evangelist almost fainting where she stood. They wanted to build temples in our honor, while all we wanted them to do was make their hearts temples unto God.

Multitudes of sick men and women and children have been brought to the meetings. In answer to believing prayer, we have seen the blind receive their sight, deaf and dumb spirits cast out so that the people both spoke and heard, the lame made to walk. Tumors, cancers, and goiters have melted like snow before the sun. Many preach this Christ as the Great "I Was." We have learned to know and preach Him as the Great "I AM," who is the same yesterday, today, and forever.

—*Aimee Semple McPherson*
1966

Lord, thank You for the great I AM—Jesus—who is the same today, yesterday . . . always . . . miracles and all! In Jesus' name. Amen.

The Personal Testimony of Aimee Semple McPherson (Los Angeles, CA: The Heritage Committee, 1966). Used by permission of the Heritage Department of the Foursquare Gospel.

Day 2

A Great Home-Going

READ 2 TIMOTHY 4:5–8

On the evening of September 26, 1944, Aimee Semple McPherson preached her last sermon before a packed crowd in Oakland, California . . . the same city where twenty-two years earlier she had received the vision of the Foursquare Gospel.

Her son explained: "Mother was suffering from a very serious kidney ailment and was under a doctor's care. He had prescribed sleeping tablets. The coroner stated clearly to me the sleeping tablets would not have had the disastrous effect if it had not been for the kidney ailment which allowed this compound to go through her system. Having been there in the room at that time, I am convinced it was God's time to take her. She had served several lifetimes wrapped up in one and had undergone great strain from her illness and overwork. I feel sure God said, 'It is enough; come on up higher.'"

EDITOR'S NOTE: *This account of the last moments in the life of Evangelist Aimee Semple McPherson is taken from her book,* The Personal Testimony of Aimee Semple McPherson.

—*Aimee Semple McPherson*
1966

Lord, thank You for faithful servants like Aimee Semple McPherson—lives whose shining examples still speak to us, even beyond the grave. In Jesus' name. Amen.

Day 3
God's Purpose for Those Fleas

READ ECCLESIASTES 3:1–11

As the days wore on the prisoners in Barracks 28 discovered that there was an astonishing lack of supervision or interference. Corrie and Betsie ten Boom used the unprecedented freedom to talk to the other prisoners, read the Bible to them, and minister in a myriad of ways. Then one day a supervisor tipped her hand as to why they were given so much latitude. "That place is crawling with fleas," the supervisor said. "I wouldn't step through the door!"

Corrie's mind rushed back to their first hour in the barracks and to their rueful prayer thanking God for fleas. When she looked up, Betsie was chuckling, her eyes sparkling. "So now we know why we were supposed to praise Him even for fleas. Even the fleas had to be His instruments for our good."

—*Catherine Marshall LeSourd*
n.d.

Lord, I thank You for wonderful testimonies like that of Corrie ten Boom—testimonies that will prompt me to give thanks in all things too. In Jesus' name. Amen.

Something More (n.p., n.d.).

Day 4
Gold of Ophir

READ PHILIPPIANS 3:8; REVELATION 3:18; PSALM 19

One of the interpretations of the Hebrew roots of the words "gold of Ophir" may be "gold of ashes." "Gold tried in the fire," as Revelation 3:18 states; we are counseled to "buy" it of Him. It comes high. It cost Paul "all things."

Dawns a day when comes the King
Every tongue His praise shall sing,
Then I stand upon His right,
Lo! I stand, O dazzling sight!
Clad in gold of Ophir!

—*Dr. Lillian B. Yeomans*
1940

Lord, burn away the dross so that from the ashes comes gold! In Jesus' name. Amen.

The Hiding Place (Springfield, MO: Gospel Publishing House, 1940).

Day 5

When God Takes Us Deeper

READ 1 KINGS 17

When God wants us to take a deeper step in Him, He will allow the wonderful experience of ours to dry up. He will withhold the rain, and there will be no power, only as we move on. This brook that once fed and nourished us will not be the food for us now. Elijah drank from this brook, but when it was God's time for him to move forward, he was obedient to the Spirit's voice.

God didn't want him to stay where there was no rain or power. As long as there was power or water in the brook, it was all right to stay; but now He wants you to go where there is rain.

—Mrs. Robert A. Brown
July 1920

Lord, thank You that You are leading me deeper and deeper, onward, where there is rain. In Jesus' name. Amen.

Weekend

Stand Still

READ EXODUS 14

In the face of the Red Sea, God commanded the people to "stand still." It is just when a man has no fear, no care, no press, no hurry, no difficulty, that he stands still. "He that is entered into his rest, he also hath ceased from his own works, as God did from His" Heb. 4:10).

"Stand still!" This meant complete confidence in God, an absence of all apprehension. The priests were to be the leaders; if they could stand perfectly still, then the people would feel there was nothing to fear.

—*Mrs. Mary Baxter*
1887

Lord, I stand still before You, trusting You to take me through. In Jesus' name. Amen.

God's People (London: Christian Herald, 1887).

Week 49—Day 1
Restored Glory

READ PSALM 84:11; HAGGAI 2:9; JOHN 17:22

The Son of God declared, "The glory which Thou gavest Me I have given them." This restored glory is for every one of His saints. Believe the record that He has restored that which He took not away. It is written of old, "The Lord will give grace." He has given grace. Grace and truth come by Jesus Christ.

But it is further written, "He will give grace and glory." He has restored the glory. The day will come when all those who are His will be transfigured. He was transfigured on the Mount, and His glory was seen. His glory will be seen in all His saints. The secret of this glory is Christ within, the hope of God. The glorious Christ of God indwelling the temple, giving a greater glory than the first Adam ever knew.

—*Hattie Hammond*
March 1938

Lord, thank You for the promise of Your glory. In Jesus' name. Amen.

"Complete Restoration," *The Pentecostal Evangel.*

Day 2

Resurrection Rays

READ PHILIPPIANS 3:10

Resurrection rays! Can you see them?
  Streaming straight from heaven above!
Resurrection rays! Do you feel them?
  Tokens of a Saviour's love.

Resurrection rays! Hallelujah!
  Lo, He maketh all things new!
Resurrection rays! Through eternal days!
  Resurrection rays for you.

—Dr. Lillian B. Yeomans
June 1930

*Lord, thank You for Your resurrection power. May I
come to understand its application in my daily walk
with You. In Jesus' name. Amen.*

Day 3

A Heart for America

READ LEVITICUS 26:3–6

Since Christ appeared to me in the night, my heart is broken for the needs of America. The burden of God's people and the multitude of unsaved is upon me in a greater way than I have ever known it in life before. Many times my spirit is so broken, I preach and pour out my heart in crying and tears.

The Spirit is crying for God's people to be revived, for sinners to be saved, and for people to be delivered from their diseases. Our great, unchanging Lord waits to come forth in signs and wonders and mighty miracles this very hour. I am praying that the cities of America shall once again be stirred.

—*Louise Nankivell*
December 1944

Lord, I pray for America. Bless our leaders, Lord; turn their hearts toward You. Forgive us, revive us, and use us as light to all nations. In Jesus' name. Amen.

"Revival Is Coming," *The Pentecostal Evangel.*

Day 4
The Bride

READ 1 CORINTHIANS 15:51–57

His chosen Bride, ordained with Him
To reign o'er all the earth;
Must be formed, ere Israel know
Her Savior's matchless worth.

Hark to the trump! Behold it breaks
The sleep of ages now,
And lo! The light of glory shines
On many an aching brow.

The scattered sons of Israel's race,
That trumpet's sound shall bring
Back to their land; to know and own
Messiah, as their King!"

—*Item in* The Latter Rain Evangel
March 1926

Lord, come quickly! In Jesus' name. Amen.

Day 5
We Are His Temple

READ 1 CORINTHIANS 3:16–23

Oh, that God's people may realize that it is not a light thing to be healed by the Lord and to have His life filling their mortal bodies!

A body healed in this way is a most sacred thing, and as we realize that we are temples of the Holy Ghost, we are to be very careful where we take these bodies, and for what purpose our strength is used.

—Carrie Judd Montgomery
1976

Lord, thank You for filling me with the Holy Spirit. Help me to realize at all times that I am Your temple, and to take care where I take You. In Jesus' name. Amen.

"Some of the Hindrances to Healing," *The Pentecostal Evangel.*

Weekend

True Faith

READ 1 CORINTHIANS 16:13; 1 THESSALONIANS 3:7–13

True faith is very bold, and says, "I will not let You go except You bless me!" This faith comes through the light of the Spirit upon the Word of God, when we are walking obediently before Him. He wants to prove more and more the riches of His grace on all lines, for the promises of God are unto us yea and amen in Christ Jesus, "unto the glory of God by us."

—*Carrie Judd Montgomery*
n.d.

Lord, please give me boldness, by Your Spirit, to stand fast in the faith. In Jesus' name. Amen.

"Some of the Hindrances to Healing," *The Pentecostal Evangel.*

Week 50—Day 1
Seven "Minds"

READ PROVERBS 4:20–27

There are seven things Christians should "mind:"

1. *Mind your tongue!* Do not let it speak hasty, cruel, or wicked words.
2. *Mind your eyes!* Do not permit them to look on wicked books, pictures, or objects.
3. *Mind your ears!* Do not suffer them to listen to wicked speeches, songs, or words.
4. *Mind your lips!* Do not let tobacco foul them, strong drink pass them, or food of the glutton enter them.
5. *Mind your hands!* Do not let them steal or fight, or write any evil words.
6. *Mind your feet!* Do not let them walk in the steps of the wicked.
7. *Mind your heart!* Do not let the love of sin dwell in it; do not give it to Satan, but ask Jesus to make it His throne.

—*Item from* Word and Work
n.d.

Jesus, help me to always mind these things. In Jesus' name. Amen.

Day 2
A Heavenly Vision

READ JOEL 2:18–27

Recently Sister Lydia Paino of Indianapolis, Indiana, told of a vision to a few at General Council: As she felt the translating power of God come over her, she was conscious of her feelings of unworthiness. But she suddenly realized that she had been caught up to be with the Lord, and was saying over and over again, "I have made it! I have made it! I have made it!"

Then she realized *why* she had received the desire of her heart; the Father's love had covered her failures and mistakes. As a father pities his children, so our heavenly Father pities them that fear Him.

—*Mayme F. Williams*
November 1939

Lord, thank You that You love me right through my failures and mistakes. Help me to love others with that same unconditional love. In Jesus' name. Amen.

"Visions of Christ's Coming," *The Pentecostal Evangel.*

Day 3
Rend Thy Garments

READ 2 KINGS 2:9–14

Before Elisha put on the mantle of Elijah, he rent his own clothes in two pieces. And the only way in which we as a church or an individual can successfully put on the wonder-working mantle of the Holy Spirit is to first rend our own garments—our own plans, methods, ideas, desires, schemes, red tape, regulations, rules—in two pieces, and strip them away. Then we may put on the mantle of power which our Lord has sent down, and which lies within reach of all who will pay the price and go all the way with Jesus.

As we rend our robes in two pieces, we cry, "Good-bye!" to our own manmade plannings and ponderings, our futile efforts of the flesh, our forming of committees to get up concerts, entertainments, or suppers to bring people to church, our thinking and scheming as to how to get sensational subjects to hold the crowds; "Good-bye" to manmade strivings to work up a revival in our own strength. As we take up the mantle of power, we are clothed with the Spirit, and cry, "Welcome, Holy Spirit! Have Thine own way!"

—*Aimee Semple McPherson*
1923

> *Lord, I rend my own garments—put away my own plans and thoughts and desires and agendas—to put on Your mantle of power and pick up Your plan for my life. In Jesus' name. Amen.*

"The Descending Mantle," *This Is That* (Self-published, 1923). Used by permission of the Heritage Department of the Foursquare Gospel.

Day 4
Tobacco

READ 1 CORINTHIANS 6:19–20; 9:24–27

Dr. Connor, formerly of Johns Hopkins Hospital, says:

> Hundreds of thousands who smoke and chew and who believe themselves healthy are suffering from progressive organic ailments. They would never have been afflicted if it had not been for the use of tobacco, and most of them would soon get well if they would only stop the use of tobacco. The best-known habit-forming principle of tobacco is nicotine, but most deadly and demoralizing is furfural. Both are deadly poisons which, when absorbed into the system, slowly but surely affect the nerves, tissues, vital organs, and vitality of the body.
>
> If you feel that you must smoke and chew to quiet your nerves, you are a slave of the tobacco habit, and are slowly poisoning yourself with the insidious deadly drugs, nicotine and furfural. In either case, you have just two alternatives: keep on poisoning yourself, regardless of the consequences, or rid yourself of the habit and escape the danger.

—*Item in* Word and Work
August 1922

Lord, break any habits that would bind or addict me to anything; set me free, by the power of the Holy Spirit. In Jesus' name. Amen.

Day 5

As!

READ ISAIAH 66:13; PSALM 19:5; 103:13; 1 THESSALONIANS 2:7;
EZEKIEL 34:12; MATTHEW 23:37; DEUTERONOMY 32:11

"As" is a vast, yet little word. Applied to salvation, how simple and how glorious. "As Moses lifted up the serpent . . . " Applied to our sins, "As far as the East is from the West." But these seven—how beautifully they speak of the touching tenderness of our God:

1. "As a mother comforteth . . . "
2. "As a father pitieth . . . "
3. "As a nurse cherisheth . . . "
4. "As a shepherd seeketh . . . "
5. "As a hen gathereth . . . "
6. "As an eagle fluttereth . . . "
7. "As a bridegroom rejoiceth . . . "

Only one word of two letters, yet how comprehensive! They are the Christian's lullaby!

—*Item in* The Pentecostal Evangel
September 1943

Lord, I praise You for the many ways You express that tiny word, "as," and for Your love and tenderness toward me. Amen.

Weekend

"Surrender! Surrender!"

READ PSALM 108

Some of you have said to me: "Why every service do you say, 'Surrender! Surrender!'"? Every meeting, you have said, 'Consecrate! Surrender! Abandon!' You just keep saying that. What do you mean? I've surrendered; I've given myself to God. I'm saved. I'm baptized in the Spirit. I'm working for the Lord and waiting for Jesus to come. Isn't that all there is to it?"

Honey, that isn't all there is to it! You haven't lived yet. Do you know that you can be saved, baptized in the Holy Spirit, and have all the gifts? You can have ten trances and ten visions and sixteen prostrations, and still not have come to the real purpose of God for your life. It is a marvelous plan, with a marvelous purpose. You'll never come into that plan until you give God your heart—all of your heart.

—*Hattie Hammond*
n.d.

Lord, I surrender! I give You my heart—all of it! Now reveal Your plan and lead me into all that You have purposed for me. In Jesus' name. Amen.

Audiocassette titled "Give Me Your Heart," from a chapel service at Christ for the Nations.

Week 51—Day 1
"What Is Eating You"

READ MARK 4:14–20

A leading medical authority says, "You do not get ulcers from what you eat. You get ulcers from what is eating you!" Another prominent authority states, "Worry affects the nerves of your stomach and actually changes the gastric juices from normal to abnormal, often leading to stomach ulcers. Worry causes nervous breakdowns, diabetes, heart trouble."

Moreover, it promotes physical weakness, exhaustion, sleeplessness, loss of appetite, and other dire consequences. Jesus knew the folly of worry and instructed us not to be anxious about what we should eat, drink, or wear—not even about the problems of another day. The Lord has promised that if we cast our burdens upon Him, He will sustain us.

—*Louise Nankivell*
January 1957

Jesus, help me to always cast my cares upon You. Amen.

"A Destructive Triad," *The Voice of Healing*.

Day 2
Only One Thing to Do

READ 1 KINGS 19:9–21

When you receive the Pentecostal experience, do not think that now the devil is going to leave you alone, and that henceforth, all will be a bed of roses. Do not forget that God has by no means finished His dealings with you. There will still be other winds, earthquakes, and fires, for if we are not careful to walk in the Spirit the flesh will be revived.

In this event what shall we do? There is only one thing to do; go back to Horeb, "the mountain of God," back to Pentecost. Hide yourself alone in the cave with God, and there wait till once more the still small voice speaks, for only then may you know that all is well between you and your God.

—Helen Ramsay
August 1930

Lord, thank You that You are not yet finished with me! Help me to get alone with You to find out what it is that You are doing right now in my life. In Jesus' name. Amen.

"Cleansing From Sin," *The Pentecostal Evangel.*

Day 3

The Features of Jesus

READ 2 CORINTHIANS 3:12–18

It would be well for us if we could imitate that beautiful man of God, Bishop Whipple, who said: "For the last forty years I have been trying to see the features of Jesus Christ in every man that differs from me."

—*Item in* The Pentecostal Evangel
August 1930

Lord, may I see Jesus in the faces of others who differ from me! In Jesus' name. Amen.

"Charity," *The Pentecostal Evangel.*

Day 4
Faith's Song

READ PSALM 57:1–3

I would be quiet, Lord,
Not tease nor fret;
Not one small need of mine
Wilt Thou forget.

—*Item in* The Pentecostal Evangel
January 1940

Lord, increase my trust in You, so that it will become against my Christ nature to worry. I cast all care on You. In Jesus' name. Amen.

Day 5

A Word to Weary Workers

READ ECCLESIASTES 11:1; ISAIAH 33:15–16

You are casting your bread upon the waters in faith, and you shall find it after many days. There is that scattereth and yet increaseth. You scatter, and you are bound to get the increase. He that goeth forth and weepeth, bearing precious seed, shall doubtless come again with rejoicing, bring his sheaves with him. He shall multiply the seed sown.

You look at the apparent waste of labor, at the seeming loss, at that which looks like failure. In His kingdom there is no loss; that which is sent forth in faith is never lost. His Word shall not return unto Him void. Therefore, be ye steadfast, unmoveable, always abounding in the work of the Lord, knowing that your labor is not in vain in the Lord. This is the Word of the living God, though circumstances seemingly contradict. Heaven and earth may pass away, but the Word of the living God abideth. When the shaking takes place, the Word of God, and the fruit of the Word, will be the one thing not shaken.

—*Item in* The Pentecostal Evangel
October 1921

> *Lord, I praise You for these encouraging words from long ago, penned as if just moments ago. Because these words are based upon Your Word, they are timeless! Strengthen me and help me to go on. In Jesus' name. Amen.*

Weekend

Stop Worrying

READ PHILIPPIANS 4:13; 2 CORINTHIANS 12:8–10

Worry is the beginning of discouragement, and discouragement spells failure.

Failure is just what Satan wants us to have, for then he soon gets advantage of us. So I say, "Stop worrying, stop yourself. Do not say you can't, for you can do all things through Christ strengthening you!"

—Mrs. G. F. Engblom
November 1925

Lord, I admit it! Sometimes I find myself worrying; please help me to stop it, and cast all care upon You! In Jesus' name. Amen.

"The Place of Worry in the Christian Life," *The Pentecostal Evangel.*

Week 52—Day 1
"I Can Hear! Hear! Hear!"

READ ISAIAH 35:4–10

When I was a little girl, about five years of age, I had a terrible sickness, and it left me stone deaf. I had to read the lips and watch the mouths of people who spoke in order to understand. I made a profession of religion, but had not enjoyed the experience that I should, and it was not until Dr. Price held that wonderful meeting in Klamath Falls that I really found the Lord.

Deaf as I was, I went to the altar and for the first time really felt the power of God. Then one night it came my turn to be anointed and prayed for. How glorious! The power of God came upon me and down I went. My heart felt so light and I was so happy. Then a terrible pain went through my head. It was awful; I could hardly stand it. Then something popped, with a loud bang in my ears. Then I heard. Oh, praise the Lord! I could hear singing and talking! I could hear every word that Dr. Price said! I could hear! Hear! Hear!

—Mrs. Phoebe Akers
March 1926

Jesus, thank You for Your miracle-working power, and that You still perform them today. Amen.

"All for His Glory," *Golden Grain.*

Day 2
The Praise Zone

READ PSALM 86:12–17; MARK 11:24

Jesus says, "What things soever you desire, when you pray, believe that ye receive them, and ye shall have them." Now, if we ask God to give us a certain answer to prayer, and proceed to believe we have it, it is only polite to begin to thank Him for it. In other words, shoot straight upward through the prayer zone into the praise zone, and thank God beforehand that according to His Word, it is done.

When contending with sickness, trouble, misunderstanding, discouragement, or depression, begin to see Jesus. Praise Him with all your heart, and the upward flight of His praises will lift you as with the wings of a great eagle above the woes of this earth.

—*Aimee Semple McPherson*
1923

Lord, thank You for the praise zone—where I can say,
by faith, "It is done!" In Jesus' name. Amen.

"Praising the Lord," *This Is That* (Self-published, 1923). Used by permission of the Heritage Department of the Foursquare Gospel.

Day 3
Just Come to Jesus

READ JOHN 14:16–18; 20:22

If you would be filled with the Holy Spirit, it is not necessary to struggle and strive and agonize before God. Just come like a simple, trusting, yielding little child. Be washed in the blood, surrender heart, mind, and voice, and your entire being to God in glad praise and submission.

Remember that He is more willing to give than we are to receive, and let Him fill your soul.

—*Carrie Judd Montgomery*
n.d.

Lord, fill me with the Holy Spirit. In Jesus' name. Amen.

Triumphs of Faith.

Day 4
"I Will Bless Thee"

READ PSALM 23:4

For the year before me God is keeping
Glad surprises, token of His love;
Let me then look up in expectation,
Watching for the blessing from above;
He who sits in power upon the throne,
He will never disappoint His own.

For the days to come I fear no evil
Thou art with me, Lord—that is enough . . .
Nothing need disturb me, naught can dim
Eyes that rest expectantly on Him!

Upon Thee my trustful gaze is turning,
Brother-Friend, and yet Almighty Guide;
At Thy feet I rest, in silence learning
Lessons taught me by the Crucified;
Through the gate of death we learn to trace
Fairer beauty in the Master's face.

For the year before me God is planning
My part therefore is to wait and see
How He can make all things serve His purpose,
Master, make me more conformed to Thee.

—*Laura A. Barter Snow*
n.d.

*Lord, thank You that You are ever with me. Lead me
on. In Jesus' name. Amen.*

Triumphs of Faith.

Day 5
Don't Be Afraid of Change

READ ISAIAH 43:18–19; PHILIPPIANS 3:13–15

Look at the evolution of the worm which spins a cocoon and later breaks out of that cocoon to become a beautiful butterfly. What if the worm had been afraid of change? What if it had never spun the cocoon? It would have dried up and died and would never have known the wonder of being a butterfly.

Never be afraid of change. Evolve. Grow. Live.

The unknown is not a threat. It is something wonderful to be discovered by you. You will discover a world of ability in yourself as you discover the unknown.

—*Daisy Washburn Osborn*
1991

> *Lord, help me to embrace change, because You are the one who is changing me, by Your Spirit. Help me to discover the excitement of the unknown. In Jesus' name. Amen.*

New Life for Women (Tulsa, OK: OSFO Publishers, 1991).

Weekend

New Year's Wishes

READ LAMENTATIONS 3:22–25

Faith that increaseth—walking in light,
Hope that aboundeth—happy and bright,
Love that is perfect—casting out fear.
These will insure you a happy New Year.
Peace in the Savior—rest at His feet.
Smile in His countenance—radiant and sweet.
Joy in His presence—Christ ever near.
These will bring to you a happy New Year.

—*Carrie Judd Montgomery*
n.d.

*Lord, I embrace this new year ahead and praise You
for the many experiences I will have with You, as I
walk in the Spirit daily. Thank You for the year ahead!
Help me to use each day wisely. In Jesus' name, Amen.*

Triumphs of Faith.

Epilogue

An Invitation to Become a Spirit-Led Woman

You're born again. Jesus is your Savior, Lord, and Master. You have wonderful times with Him in prayer, and sometimes even sense His presence during praise and worship. Your prayers are answered, the family is doing fine, life seems to have its normal share of highs and lows—but mostly things are stable. This is good . . . *isn't it?*

Yet perhaps there's a nagging thought that something is missing in your spiritual walk—an absence of power, a lack of testimonies about the miraculous, wonder-working God of the New Testament church. Or have you wondered whether miracles, signs, and wonders have simply passed away?

You have just read the powerful life testimonies of Spirit-led women in the last century and a half who—against all odds and seemingly insurmountable obstacles—broke through barriers, overcame social taboos, crossed oceans, climbed the mountain of prayer, preached their hearts out, poured their lives out, healed the sick, raised the dead, heard God's voice, had visions of heaven, and did fabulous exploits for the Lord. Their extraordinary lives are living testaments to the fact that *Jesus never stopped performing miracles*—and that He is still performing them today. Only He uses people to pour His miracle-working power through.

Is your spiritual life so safe and stable that it lacks the

luster of excitement and adventures in Christ? *Then perhaps it's time to step out of the boat and go for it:* Pray to be filled with the Holy Spirit, so the power of God can flow out from you and touch the lives of others.

But if you do, be prepared for change, because it is this remarkable transforming power—the power of the Holy Spirit—that transformed Peter from frightened, wimpish denier of Christ to mighty Rock of apostolic works . . . transformed Saul of Tarsus from Christian-killer to church-founder . . . transformed the hundred and twenty from timid Christ-followers to mountain-moving world-shapers. Be prepared to change, for to become Spirit-filled is to become Spirit-directed . . . Spirit-led. It is to become Spirit-taught, Spirit-walking, Spirit-praying, Spirit-inspired women of God. It is to become Spirit-yielded to His marvelous plan for your life. Will you?

If you desire to be baptized in the Holy Spirit, may I suggest that you read and study the wonderful promises contained in Luke 11:5–13; Acts 1:5, 8; Acts 2:1–8; and Acts 11:16. Get to know and trust the operation of the Holy Spirit through these passages even before you pray. Rest in the knowledge that the Holy Spirit is no invader, and certainly no counterfeit Spirit; He requires your permission to baptize you in the Holy Spirit; He will not simply rush in, unless you hunger and thirst for more of Him. You are accustomed to asking Jesus for answers in prayer; *now ask Him for the Holy Spirit.* From these verses in Luke, chapter 11, you can easily see that if you ask Him for the Holy Spirit He will personally vouch for your receiving the Holy Spirit—and only the Holy Spirit. He will send exactly what you ask for—not a counterfeit.

Ask in faith to be filled with the Holy Spirit, and believe you'll receive just what you ask for. He is a glorious God who delights to fill His children with the Holy Spirit. And He will take you on adventures in prayer and in practice that will one day fill His Book in heaven.

You may pray as the Lord directs you to pray, or you may wish to pray a prayer like this:

> *Lord Jesus, thank You for saving me and for washing me in Your blood. I renounce all sin. I renounce all rebellion and disobedience. I renounce the devil and all his works, and ask that You forgive me for anything I was ever involved with that displeased or dishonored You. Jesus, I know You promised to send the Comforter when You ascended to the Father. You promised that He—the Holy Spirit—would never leave us. Now fill me, Lord, with the Holy Spirit and give me the evidence of my heavenly language. Thank You that as You fill me with the Spirit, You also begin to teach and instruct me in the deeper application of Your Word in my daily walk. Lead me to the plan You always purposed for my life. Show me how You would use me in my world to reach out to others. Develop within me the fruit of the Spirit and send the gifts of the Spirit that You wish for me to have in daily activation. Thank You, Lord, for baptizing me in the Spirit. In Jesus' name. Amen.*

God bless you richly as you enter in to this most wonderful of all life experiences.

Author Biographies

ARGUE, ZELMA—Canadian-born evangelist and teacher in the Pentecostal movement; daughter of A. H. Argue.

BAXTER, MARY—Cofounder of Bethshan Faith Home in London, England, in 1882. She was married to the editor of the *Christian Herald* in London, and her activities in Holiness and Divine Healing circles brought her to America on a frequent basis.

BEALL, MYRTLE—Pastor and founder of Bethesda Missionary Temple in Detroit, Michigan, where the Latter Rain movement started in 1948.

BOOM, CORRIE TEN—Survivor of Ravensbruck concentration camp during World War II; later wrote several books, including the best-selling *The Hiding Place*, about her experiences.

BOSWORTH, MRS. F. F. Wife of healing evangelist F. F. Bosworth.

BRANDT, ROXANNE—International author and speaker in the Charismatic movement. She conducted miracle services and crusades throughout the world.

BRITTON, ANNA D.—Church pioneer, teacher; pioneered churches throughout Southern California and Canada. She taught in the L.I.F.E. Bible School, founded L.I.F.E. Bible College in Canada, and supervised the Foursquare Canadian works.

BROWN, MRS. ROBERT (MARIE BURGESS)—Pastor, teacher, wife of Robert Brown of Northern Ireland, and cofounder and copastor of Glad Tidings Tabernacle in New York City with her husband.

COE, JUANITA—Wife of Voice of Healing evangelist Jack Coe; took over the evangelistic association after his death in 1956.

CONWAY, LELA M.—Frequent contributor to early Pentecostal periodicals such as the *Latter Rain Evangel;* based out of the State of Maryland.

CRAWFORD, FLORENCE—Founded the Apostolic Faith Mission in 1907 in Portland, Oregon; received the baptism in the Holy Spirit at Azusa Street in 1906.

DABNEY, MRS. E. J.—Wife of E. J. Dabney, who pastored a black church in the Norfolk, Virginia, area.

FLOWERS, ALICE—Wife of Pentecostal pioneer Joseph Flowers; they started the *Christian Evangel,* which later became the *Pentecostal Evangel.*

FRODSHAM, ALICE ROWLANDS—Wife of Stanley Frodsham, an early Pentecostal writer, editor, and teacher.

GARRIGUS, ALICE—Founder of the Pentecostal Assemblies of Newfoundland, Canada. She started Bethesda Mission at age fifty-two in 1910.

GOODWIN, CARMEN THACKER—Wife of Assemblies of God pastor J. R. Goodwin; known by many as "Mom and Pop Goodwin," for their unique teaching on the gifts of the Holy Spirit.

GRACE, CLARA—Teacher and evangelist; specialized in the areas of the baptism of the Holy Spirit and End-Time prophecy.

GUYON, JEANNE MARIE—French mystic who lived from 1648–1717. Widowed at age twenty-eight, her writings on the deeper life caused her to be imprisoned several times. She spent her final years doing charitable work.

HAMMOND, HATTIE—Pastor, evangelist, teacher, missionary with the Assemblies of God; called the "girl evangelist" because of manifestations of healings that took place in her meetings as a young woman. By the 1930s she was considered one of the most intense speakers in the Pentecostal movement.

HORN, EDNA JEAN—Pioneer radio broadcaster for more than fifty-seven years. She was a charter member of the National Religious Broadcasters.

KUHLMAN, KATHRYN—Pastor, healing evangelist, radio and television personality; born in Concordia, Missouri. After an unsuccessful marriage, she moved to Franklin, Pennsylvania, in 1946 and started a church. Soon after starting her radio ministry, she moved to Pittsburgh. In the 1960s she began holding crusades all over the country. She produced hundreds of television programs. She died in Tulsa, Oklahoma, in 1976.

MARSHALL, CATHERINE—Best-selling author; born in Tennessee and healed of tuberculosis as a young woman after years of suffering. In 1936 she married Peter Marshall, and after his death in 1949 she began a successful writing career. Her best-known books are *Christy*, published in 1967, and the biography of her late husband, *A Man Called Peter*, in 1951.

MCPHERSON, AIMEE SEMPLE—Missionary, pastor, healing evangelist, editor, author, and founder of the International Church of the Foursquare Gospel. In 1910 she and her husband left for China as missionaries but her husband died within weeks of their arrival in Hong Kong. Returning to the States, she met and later married Harold McPherson. In 1921 she founded Angelus Temple. She was the first woman to receive an FCC license to operate a radio station. She founded L.I.F.E. Bible College and established the Foursquare denomination.

MIX, ELIZABETH—First black female healing evangelist; healed of tuberculosis under the ministry of Ethan O. Allan. Carrie Judd Montgomery was subsequently healed through corresponding with Mrs. Mix.

MONTGOMERY, CARRIE JUDD—Writer, minister, missionary, publisher; healed of a terminal illness at a young age. She began to publish *Triumphs of Faith* in 1881 in Buffalo, New York, which she published for the next sixty-five years. She established the Home of Peace, a faith home which later became a missionary home. She was active in the Christian Missionary Alliance and The Salvation Army and in 1908 received the baptism of the Holy Spirit. She became a charter member of the Assemblies of God, and was an important link between the various Holiness denominations and the Pentecostals.

MOSS, VIRGINIA—Educator, pastor, director; healed of paralysis in 1904 and founded the Door of Hope Mission in 1906. Received the baptism of the Holy Spirit in 1907. She then opened a faith home in 1909, and later started

Beulah Heights Bible and Missionary Training School.

MURPHY, LEONA SUMRALL—Evangelist and sister of the famed missionary-evangelist, Lester Sumrall. She entered the ministry as a teenager. Stricken with muscular dystrophy as a young woman, she was miraculously healed by the power of God.

NANKIVELL, LOUISE—Evangelist with the Voice of Healing. She preached in sackcloth when conducting healing and evangelistic crusades, and many miracles took place in her meetings.

NUZUM, MRS. C.—Missionary to Mexico; wrote a series of tracts later compiled as *The Life of Faith,* still published by Gospel Publishing House.

ORMBSY, MRS. E. J.—Daughter of Maria Woodworth-Etter; assisted her mother in various church functions.

OSBORN, DAISY WASHBURN—Missionary, healing evangelist, author, women's leader. Born in California, she met T. L. Osborn in 1940 and married him the next year. After several years in ministry, the Osborns began a missionary-healing ministry that took them to forty countries.

PALMER, PHOEBE—Teacher, speaker, author; considered by many to be the "mother" of the Holiness movement.

PIPER, LYDIA MARKLEY—Wife of Pentecostal pioneer William Hamner Piper and a frequent contributor to the *Latter Rain Evangel,* started by her husband in 1908.

PRICE, MARJORIE—daughter of well-known healing evangelist, Charles Price.

REIDT, GERTRUDE—Daughter of famed teacher, John G. Lake. Along with her husband, Wilford Reidt, she specialized in teaching on intercessory prayer.

RICHEY, ELOISE MAY—Wife of healing evangelist , Raymond T. Richey.

SANFORD, AGNES—Married to an Episcopal priest, she searched the Scriptures concerning healing. Her first book, *The Healing Light,* was published in 1947 and became a best-seller. She went on to author other major books on divine healing before being baptized in the Holy Spirit in the early 1950s. She was a major promoter of the renewal of the Holy Spirit within historical churches.

SEXTON, MRS. E. A.—Editor of Pentecostal periodical, *Bridegroom Messenger.*

SISSON, ELIZABETH—Early Pentecostal pioneer, missionary, author, and evangelist; associated with Carrie Judd Montgomery and later assisted F. F. Bosworth in Dallas, Texas.

SIZELOVE, RACHEL—Baptized in the Holy Spirit at Azusa Street, she returned to Springfield, Missouri, to bring that area the message of Pentecost.

STAPLETON, RUTH CARTER—Raised Baptist, she was baptized in the Holy Spirit and became involved with the healing ministry which emphasized inner healing. Her brother was President Jimmy Carter.

WANNENMACHER, HELEN—Along with her husband, Joseph, she pioneered pastoring for the Assemblies of God.

WIGGLESWORTH, POLLY—Preacher, evangelist; saved under the ministry of The Salvation Army and married to Smith Wigglesworth in 1882. Together they started Bradford Mission. She usually did the preaching while her husband prayed with those who came to the altar.

WILKERSON, JEANNE—Teacher and prayer-group leader; born in Missouri. She had a divine passion for Christ and became deeply involved in prayer and intercession, leading a prayer group for over twenty years.

WILLITTS, ETHEL—Healing evangelist.

WOODWORTH-ETTER, MARIA—Pastor, author, healing evangelist, Pentecostal pioneer. Healings, signs, and wonders marked her meetings and increased crowds. Often she would go into trances, some lasting for hours, and was consequently known as the "trance evangelist." She made the transition into Pentecostalism because tongues were manifesting in her meetings even before Azusa Street. In 1918 she opened a church in Indianapolis, Indiana.

YEOMANS, LILLIAN B.—Medical doctor, teacher, healing evangelist, author, educator; trained as a physician, she became addicted to morphine to relieve the stress of a strenuous schedule.She entered John Alexander Dowie's Divine Healing Home in Chicago, Illinois, in 1898. There, she was delivered from drug addiction. Baptized in the Holy Spirit in 1907, she later assisted Aimee Semple McPherson in pioneering L.I.F.E. Bible School.